FISCHER MIDDLE SCHOOL

P9-BZX-547

30044000008468.   920 CUL

Weather and climate : the

PIONEERS in SCIENCE

WEATHER AND CLIMATE

The People Behind the Science

KATHERINE CULLEN, PH.D.

CHELSEA HOUSE
PUBLISHERS
An imprint of Infobase Publishing

PROPERTY OF FISCHER MIDDLE SCHOOL
1305 LONG GROVE DRIVE
AURORA, IL 60504

I dedicate this book to
all future pioneers in science.
୯ᡚ

Weather and Climate: The People behind the Science

Copyright © 2006 by Katherine Cullen, Ph.D.

All rights reserved. No part of this book may be reproduced or utilized in any form or by any means, electronic or mechanical, including photocopying, recording, or by any information storage or retrieval systems, without permission in writing from the publisher. For information contact:

Chelsea House
An imprint of Infobase Publishing
132 West 31st Street
New York NY 10001

Library of Congress Cataloging-in-Publication Data
Cullen, Katherine E.
    Weather and climate: the people behind the science / Katherine Cullen.
        p. cm. — (Pioneers in science)
    Includes bibliographical references and index.
    ISBN 0-8160-5466-5 (acid-free paper)
    1. Meteorologists—Biography—Juvenile literature. 2. Meteorologists—History—Juvenile literature. 3. Climatologists—Biography—Juvenile literature.
4. Climatologists—History—Juvenile literature. I. Title. II. Series.
    QC858.A2C85 2006
    551.5'092'2—dc22   2004030604

Chelsea House books are available at special discounts when purchased in bulk quantities for businesses, associations, institutions, or sales promotions. Please call our Special Sales Department in New York at (212) 967-8800 or (800) 322-8755.

You can find Chelsea House on the World Wide Web at http://www.chelseahouse.com

Text design by Mary Susan Ryan-Flynn
Cover design by Cathy Rincon
Illustrations by Bobbi McCutcheon

Printed in the United States of America

MP FOF 10 9 8 7 6 5 4 3 2 1

This book is printed on acid-free paper.

CONTENTS

Preface   vii
Acknowledgments   xi
Introduction   xiii

CHAPTER 1
Evangelista Torricelli (1608–1647): Inventor of the Mercury Barometer   1

Galileo's Assistant   2
The Invention of the Barometer   3
Contributions to Mathematics   6
How a Thermometer Works   6
A Premature Ending   9
Chronology   9
Further Reading   10

CHAPTER 2
Benjamin Franklin (1706–1790): Lightning As an Electrical Phenomenon   11

The Family Business   12
Printing Apprentice   13
On His Own   14
Poor Richard's Almanack   15
The Pennsylvania Fireplace   16
Experiments with Electricity   18
So What Actually Happened?   20
Studies on Whirlwinds and the Gulf Stream   21
A Founder of a New Nation   23

Chronology   24
Further Reading   25

CHAPTER 3
Luke Howard (1772–1864): Classification of Cloud Types   27
Watching the Sky   28
Science in His Spare Time   28
On the Modification of Clouds   29
Cloud Formation   *32*
Authority on Meteorology   34
Modern Cloud Classification   35
Chronology   37
Further Reading   38

CHAPTER 4
Sir Francis Beaufort (1774–1857): Establishment of a
Scale for Wind Force   41
False Records   42
A Passion for Sea Life   43
The Need for Standard Weather Reporting   45
What Moves the Air and the Water?   *46*
A More Precise Scale   47
International Scale Adoption   48
Matthew Fontaine Maury   *50*
Beaufort's Legacy   51
Chronology   52
Further Reading   53

CHAPTER 5
Louis Agassiz (1807–1873): Proof for the Existence of a
Great Ice Age   55
Assistant to Cuvier   56
Studies on Glaciers   58
Glaciers   *59*
Resistance   61
How the Motions of the Earth Affect Its Climate   *64*
A One-Way Trip to the United States   66

A Foundation for Paleoclimatology   68
Chronology   70
Further Reading   71

CHAPTER 6
William Ferrel (1817–1891): Effect of the Earth's Rotation
on Atmospheric and Oceanic Circulation   73

Mathematics on a Barn Door   74
The Newton of Meteorology   75
Tides   76
The Effect of Rotation on Moving Bodies   77
Tide-Predicting Machine   79
Coriolis Effect   80
Chronology   83
Further Reading   84

CHAPTER 7
John Tyndall (1820–1893): The Effect of Invisible
Gases on the Earth's Temperature   87

Surveyor, Lecturer, Fellow   88
Glacial Motion   89
Father of the Greenhouse Theory   90
Radiant Heat   90
Why the Sky Is Blue   92
Foghorns   94
The Defeat of Spontaneous Generation   94
Popularization of Natural Philosophy   95
Chronology   97
Further Reading   98

CHAPTER 8
Cleveland Abbe (1838–1916): America's First Weatherman   99

Dreams of Astronomy   100
From Russia to Washington   101
The Daily Weather Bulletin   101
Creation of a National Weather Service   104
A Matter of Time   105

Time Measurement 106
A Useful Servant 107
Chronology 109
Further Reading 110

CHAPTER 9
Vilhelm Bjerknes (1862–1951): The Movement of Air Masses in the Atmosphere 113

A Father's Influence 114
Physical Hydrodynamics 115
An Ambitious Program 116
Battle in the Atmosphere 117
Jacob Bjerknes 118
Father of Modern Meteorology 124
Chronology 125
Further Reading 126

CHAPTER 10
Paul J. Crutzen (1933–   ): Depletion of the Ozone Layer 129

Hardships 130
A Second Career 131
Mario J. Molina 134
SSTs and Anthropogenic Chlorine 136
Hole in the Ozone 137
Biomass Burning and Nuclear Winter 138
Honors and Impact 140
Chronology 141
Further Reading 143

Glossary 145
Further Resources 151
Index 157

PREFACE

Being first in line earns a devoted fan the best seat in the stadium. The first runner to break the ribbon spanning the finish line receives a gold medal. The firstborn child inherits the royal throne. Certain advantages or privileges often accompany being the first, but sometimes the price paid is considerable. Neil Armstrong, the first man to walk on the Moon, began flying lessons at age 16, toiled at numerous jobs to pay tuition, studied diligently to earn his bachelor's degree in aerospace engineering, flew 78 combat missions in Korea as a brave navy pilot, worked as a civilian test pilot for seven years, then as an astronaut for NASA for another seven years, and made several dangerous trips into space before the historic *Apollo 11* mission. He endured rigorous physical and mental preparation, underwent years of training, and risked his life to courageously step foot where no man had ever walked before. Armstrong was a pioneer of space exploration; he opened up the way for others to follow. Not all pioneering activities may be as perilous as space exploration. But like the ardent fan, a pioneer in science must be dedicated; like the competitive runner, she must be committed; and like being born to royalty, sometimes providence plays a role.

Science encompasses all knowledge based on general truths or observed facts. More narrowly defined, science refers to a branch of knowledge that specifically deals with the natural world and its laws. Philosophically described, science is an endeavor, a search for truth, a way of knowing, or a means of discovering. Scientists gain information through employing a procedure called the scientific method. The scientific method requires one to state the problem and formulate a testable hypothesis or educated guess to describe a phenomenon or explain an observation, test the hypothesis experimentally or by collecting data from observations, and draw conclusions from the results. Data can eliminate a hypothesis, but never confirm it with absolute certainty; scientists may accept a hypothesis as true when sufficient supporting evidence has been obtained. The process sounds entirely straightforward, but sometimes advancements in science do not follow such a logical approach. Because humans make the observations, generate the hypothesis, carry out the experiments, and draw the conclusions, students of science must recognize the personal dimension of science.

Pioneers in Science is a set of volumes that profile the people behind the science, individuals who initiated new lines of thought or research. They risked possible failure and often faced opposition but persisted to pave new pathways of scientific exploration. Their backgrounds vary tremendously; some never graduated from secondary school, while others earned multiple advanced degrees. Familial affluence allowed some to pursue research unhindered by financial concerns, but others were so poor they suffered from malnutrition or became homeless. Personalities ranged from exuberant to somber and gentle to stubborn, but they all sacrificed, giving their time, insight, and commitment because they believed in the pursuit of knowledge. The desire to understand kept them going when they faced difficulties, and their contributions moved science forward.

The set consists of eight separate volumes: *Biology; Chemistry; Earth Science; Marine Science; Physics; Science, Technology, and Society; Space and Astronomy;* and *Weather and Climate*. Each book contains 10 biographical sketches of pioneering individuals in a subject, including information about their childhood, how they entered into their scientific careers, their research, and enough background science information for the reader to appreciate their discoveries and contributions. Though all the profiled individuals are certainly distinguished, their inclusion is not intended to imply that they are the greatest scientists of all time. Rather, the profiled individuals were selected to reflect a variety of subdisciplines in each field, different histories, alternative approaches to science, and diverse characters.

Each chapter includes a chronology and a list of specific references about the individual and his work. Each book also includes an introduction to the field of science to which its pioneers contributed, line illustrations, photographs, a glossary of scientific terms related to the research described in the text, and a listing of further resources for information about the general subject matter.

The goal of this set is to provide, at an appropriate level, factual information about pioneering scientists. The authors hope that readers will be inspired to achieve greatness themselves, to feel connected to the people behind science, and to believe that they may have a positive and enduring impact on society.

ACKNOWLEDGMENTS

I would like to thank Frank K. Darmstadt, Executive Editor of science and mathematics at Infobase Publishing, for his skillful guidance and extreme patience, and to Melissa Cullen-DuPont, for having all the answers. Appreciation is also extended to illustrator Bobbi McCutcheon for her dedicated professionalism, to Ann E. Hicks for her constructive suggestions, and to Amy L. Conver at Facts On File, Inc., for her copyediting skills. The reference librarians and support staff of the main branch of the Medina County District Library, located in Medina, Ohio, deserve acknowledgment for their assistance in obtaining interlibrary loans, acquiring numerous special requests, and handling the hundreds of materials and resources the author borrowed during the writing of this set. Gratitude is also expressed to Pam Shirk, former media specialist at A. I. Root Middle School in Medina, Ohio, for sharing her expertise. Many people and organizations generously gave permission to use their photographs. Their names are acknowledged underneath the donated images. Thank you all.

INTRODUCTION

According to folklore, "when dew is on the grass, rain will never come to pass," "when the Sun sets unhappily with a red veiled face, then will the morning be angry with wind and storm," "cats scratch a post before wind, wash their faces before a rain, and sit with backs to the fire before snow," and the number of chirps made in 14 seconds by a grasshopper lying on the cool ground indicates the temperature. Though jokes deriding the ability of *meteorologists* to correctly predict the *weather* are commonplace, the advanced level of scientific knowledge in combination with the availability of modern technology has greatly improved weather forecasting compared with the former methods. Weather is the condition of the air surrounding a particular area at a certain time and includes references to temperature, humidity, wind speeds, cloudiness, and precipitation. The concept of *climate* refers to general weather conditions occurring in a defined area over an extended period of time.

Whether one approaches atmospheric science from a global or a local scale, the principles of physics and chemistry figure prominently in understanding factors that affect the weather and climate of the planet. Heat energy from the Sun is responsible for warming the Earth's atmosphere, but due to the spherical shape of the planet, different regions are warmed to different degrees and at different times. The equatorial region is closest to the Sun and therefore receives more direct radiation than the poles, resulting in air masses over different areas of the globe having different temperatures. As the Earth orbits the Sun, it rotates on its tilted axis; these movements contribute to variations in temperature over the time-span of a day, a calendar year, and even periods of thousands of years. Warmth from the Sun transforms water from the oceans and other water bodies into vapor that rises and adds moisture to the atmosphere. When the moisture-laden air rises further and cools, that moisture condenses into clouds from which precipitation falls. Molecules comprising the atmosphere also significantly influence the Earth's climate by absorbing radiation, trapping heat, and reflecting radiation both back into space and back toward the Earth. Pressure effects come into play as warm air that is less dense than cold air rises while the relatively colder, denser air sinks. All these factors lead to the formation of bodies of air with different physical properties and therefore, the formation of fronts, the boundaries where air masses with different properties meet. Fronts explain weather phenomena such as thunderstorms and cyclones. Winds develop when masses of air that have different pressures meet and the molecules struggle to achieve equilibrium by rushing from the mass with higher pressure toward the mass with lower pressure.

The major goal of *meteorology*, the study of the Earth's weather, is to understand the interaction of all the factors that produce the weather to be able to predict weather conditions. As well as working to improve their ability to forecast dangerous weather events, meteorologists presently are investigating methods of controlling the weather to prevent potentially destructive conditions, such as seeding artificial rainfall to tame a violent hurricane. One important question *climatologists* currently are addressing is "What effect do people have on the global climate?" Related to this issue is the trend of rising levels of greenhouse gases in the atmosphere and how this will affect the average global temperature in the coming years.

The word "meteorology" comes from *Meteorologica*, the title of a book written by the ancient Greek philosopher Aristotle in 350 BCE. Aristotle proposed that the Sun's heat caused moisture to rise into the air, where it cooled, and then returned to the Earth as rain. By that time people already were recording basic weather data such as the amount of rainfall, but contributions to understanding the weather were only piecemeal until the 19th century. Progress was sluggish, and scientists did not recognize meteorology as a scientific subject until the 20th century. Because of that perception, most brilliant young scientists trained in physics and chemistry did not consider the field of meteorology a worthy endeavor, which in turn, hampered its development into a respected discipline.

Those who were interested in atmospheric phenomena lacked suitable instruments for examination. Atmospheric pressure is one of the most basic features in studies of weather and climate; the Italian mathematician Evangelista Torricelli invented the mercury barometer for measuring atmospheric pressure in 1643. The first reliable tool for measuring temperature was not available until 1724, when Daniel Gabriel Fahrenheit described the use of mercury in place of alcohol in thermometers. In 1752, when Benjamin Franklin demonstrated that lightning was a discharge of electricity, he replaced some of the mystery shadowing weather by showing that its phenomena were not supernatural miracles but that they could be explained scientifically. The Englishman Luke Howard described a system for classifying clouds in 1802, providing an objective means to exchange ideas about atmospheric conditions, and he published a book, *Seven Lectures in Meteorology* (1837), that is considered the first meteorology textbook. By that time, amateur meteorologists had the means to assess and describe some aspects of weather conditions with a degree of objectivity, but the means of conveying the characteristics of wind were still extremely subjective, hampering effective communication between sailors and others who lives depended on safe nautical travel. The Irish hydrographer Sir Francis Beaufort recognized the need for standardized weather reporting and devised a scale for wind force that was adopted internationally.

The climate of Europe was temperate during the 19th century, similar to how it is today and to how it has been as far back as history recorded. Ten thousand years ago, however, much of the Northern Hemisphere was covered by massive sheets of ice. The Swiss-born naturalist Louis Agassiz used geological data to reveal evidence of a historical ice age, demonstrating that the Earth's climate undergoes significant changes over time. The motion of the Earth is one factor that affects local and seasonal climate variations. William Ferrel mathematically described fluid circulation patterns as they related to the atmosphere and the oceans. The Irish natural philosopher John Tyndall related changes in climate to fluctuations in atmospheric gases, specifically, levels of water vapor and carbon dioxide that affected the transmission of radiant heat.

In 1869, Cleveland Abbe started his *Daily Weather Bulletin,* an event that marked the commencement of daily weather reporting for the general public, a practice on which modern society depends. Even after Abbe created the U.S. National Weather Bureau (now the National Weather Service), forecasting the weather remained an exercise in speculation until the Norwegian physicist Vilhelm Bjerknes transformed it into a science by explaining the movement of air masses in the atmosphere as the consequence of the natural action of physical laws. Bjerknes's research into the behavior of air masses and the characteristics of fronts evolved into the theories that form the foundation of modern meteorology. Current issues relating to weather and climate, such as the effect of human activities on the atmosphere, have attracted the interest of honored scientists such as Paul Crutzen, who earned a Nobel Prize in chemistry for his research into processes that deplete the Earth's protective ozone layer.

In the nature of science, finding the answers to some questions only leads to more. The pioneers profiled in this book tenaciously strived to make sense of the marvels that take place in the Earth's atmosphere, modern scientists venture to answer the new questions raised by their predecessors, and future atmospheric scientists and climatologists will master the challenges that today's research presents. Just as the global climate cycles through periods when glaciers abound and periods of relative warmth, the cycle of science continues as scientists figure out how to explain some phenomena and subsequently reveal more unanswered questions.

Evangelista Torricelli

(1608–1647)

Evangelista Torricelli was a mathematician famous for inventing the barometer. (*Science Photo Library/Photo Researchers, Inc.*)

Inventor of the Mercury Barometer

Though invisible, *air* has mass; therefore gravity pulls it downward toward the Earth's surface, giving it weight. Everything on Earth is pressed down upon by the collective weight of all the molecules contained within a column of air reaching a height of 50 miles (80.5 km). At higher elevations, there is not as much total air above an object to weigh down upon it; thus, as altitude increases, *air pressure* decreases. Knowledge of air pressure, also called atmospheric pressure, is useful for understanding and predicting weather patterns since differences cause *winds* to develop. Meteorologists use tools called *barometers* to measure air pressure. Evangelista Torricelli (pronounced tor-ree-CHEL-lee) was a respected Italian mathematician who was a pupil of Galileo. He made important contributions to geometry, but he is most famous for his invention of the *mercury barometer.*

Galileo's Assistant

Evangelista Torricelli was the first of three sons born to Gaspare, a textile artisan, and Caterina (Angetti) Torricelli. He was born on October 15, 1608, near Faenza, Romanga, which is now part of north-central Italy. At a young age, Evangelista became an orphan, and a paternal uncle who was a monk assumed his care and education. Beginning in 1625, he studied mathematics and philosophy at the Jesuit school in Faenza. He did so well that his uncle sent him to Rome to the College di Sapienza, where Benedetto Castelli, another member of his order who specialized in mathematics and was a hydraulic engineer, supervised his education. Castelli was also a former pupil of the famous Italian physicist and astronomer Galileo Galilei, which was to be an important factor in the direction Torricelli's career eventually took. Castelli was very impressed by Torricelli's logical and creative mind and hired him as his secretary.

In 1632, Torricelli responded to a letter from Galileo on behalf of Castelli, who was traveling. In the correspondence he took the liberty of introducing himself to Galileo and not-so-modestly stated his qualifications as a knowledgeable mathematician. He also included some complimentary statements concerning a recent publication by Galileo. Torricelli's activities for the next eight years are not well documented, though there is suggestion that he served as secretary to Governor Monsignor Giovanni Ciampoli, another contemporary of Galileo. During this time Torricelli advanced his mathematics and physics research well enough to compose a treatise that clearly explained and extended Galileo's work on gravity and motion. He also applied Galileo's mechanics to the flow of fluids. While visiting Rome again in 1641, Torricelli asked Castelli for his opinion of this work, and in turn, Castelli suggested to his aging mentor, Galileo, that he hire Torricelli as an assistant to help him outline additional lectures on these subjects.

In October of 1641, Torricelli joined Galileo in Arcetri and even resided at his house. He stayed there until Galileo's death the following January. During this brief time, Galileo suggested Torricelli attempt to create a *vacuum*, a space void of everything, even air. Torricelli's acceptance of this challenge led to his fame in the field of meteorology. Historically, scientists believed that nature abhorred vacuums, an idea originating with Aristotle and referred to as *horror vacui*. This notion held that nature would do whatever was necessary to prevent a vacuum from forming or from being sustained. Galileo believed that it was the force of nature trying to avoid a vacuum that would allow a piston to raise water up a cylinder. But he was puzzled as to why the suction pumps used in mines could only raise the water about 33 feet (10 m) above its natural level. If the force of a vacuum was responsible for raising the water as Galileo believed, then why did the water not reach the top of the pumps?

The Invention of the Barometer

Torricelli had a different hypothesis than Galileo. He thought that air possessed weight, a radical idea in those days. The nature of *gases* was still mysterious, and in fact, the word "gas" had not yet been invented. If air had weight, then it could push down on the water outside the cylinder, forcing the water up as the piston was raised and created available space inside the cylinder. To test this hypothesis, Torricelli put mercury in a four-foot (1.2-m)-long glass tube closed at one end but open at the other end. He also placed some mercury, which is 13.6 times denser than water, in a bowl so there would be no way for air to pass up into the tube. Use of a lighter liquid such as water or alcohol would have demanded the tube be almost 50 feet (15 m) high to balance the weight of the *atmosphere.* Then, while holding his finger over the open end of the tube, he inverted it so that the covered end was inside the bowl. After removing his finger, the mercury began to drain out of the tube into the partially filled bowl. However, it stopped at about 30 inches (760 mm) above the surface of the mercury in the dish. As the mercury sank out of the tube, the air pressure in the top of the tube was reduced, and the weight of the external air exerted pressure on the mercury, trying to push it back into the tube and preventing it from

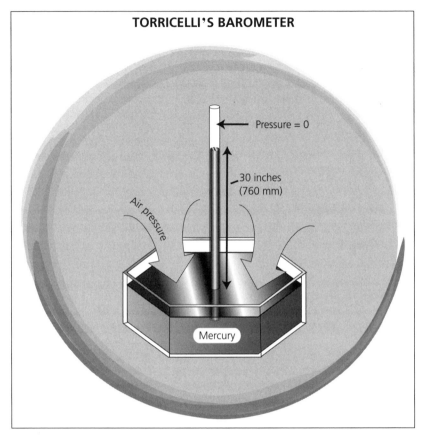

The weight of the external air presses down upon the mercury in the bowl, pushing the mercury up into the tube to a level dependent upon the air pressure.

completely emptying. This experiment proved air has weight. Torricelli repeated the procedure using a tube with a sphere at the top, showing that the volume of the vacuum had no effect on the height of the column, again demonstrating that it was an external force, not a vacuum, supporting the column of mercury. Torricelli demonstrated that the weight of the atmosphere is equivalent to that of a column of mercury 760 millimeters high. A "torr," named after Torricelli, is a unit of measure equivalent to the pressure that causes the mercury column to rise one millimeter of mercury (760 torr = 1 atmosphere of pressure = 14.7 pounds per square inch). Today scientists usually use other units such as millibars to measure barometric pressure (1 millibar = 0.750 torr).

Since there was nothing in the glass tube on top of the mercury, this famous experiment was also the first time someone created a sustained vacuum. Torricelli reportedly was interested in the effect of a vacuum on living organisms. He attempted to investigate this by introducing insects and small animals into the space containing the vacuum, but they could not survive the weight of the mercury. Torricelli also observed that light and *magnetism* could pass through a vacuum.

Returning to the question of suction pumps in mines, water could be pumped up only as far as the air pressure would allow. Greater pressure would push it up farther only until the point at which the weight of the water held up in the pump was equally balanced by the weight of the external air.

The height of the mercury column varied slightly day to day. This was due to minor natural fluctuations in the atmospheric pressure. On any given day, more or less pressure would be exerted on the surface of the mercury in the bowl. Torricelli's mercury barometer was the first instrument capable of measuring these changes, which are related to different weather conditions. His invention also initiated and facilitated a sudden increase of scientific investigations of gases and the atmosphere. Scientists devised new methods for creating vacuums and invented different types of barometers. For example, pilots use *aneroid barometers*, which do not use any fluid, to estimate the altitude of an airplane.

The French mathematician and physicist Blaise Pascal (1623–62), a friend of Torricelli's, performed an experiment providing further supporting evidence for Torricelli's hypothesis that air had weight. He inferred that if it was indeed the weight of air that supported the column of mercury to a certain height, then at higher altitudes, less air would weigh on the mercury, and the resulting column of mercury would not be as high. Too sickly to test this himself, Pascal sent two mercury barometers up a mountain with his brother-in-law and found that, indeed, the height of the column of mercury decreased as altitude increased. Pascal continued expanding Torricelli's work by observing that *precipitation* (rain or snow) often followed a drop in air pressure.

After Galileo died in 1642, Torricelli replaced him as court mathematician and philosopher to the grand duke Ferdinando II of

Tuscany (northwestern Italy). Ferdinando himself is considered a pioneer in meteorology for collecting quantitative data such as *temperature*, air pressure, and *humidity* from several nations for analysis, thus creating the first international weather-observing network. Torricelli lived in Florence and served in this capacity until his death. He was very productive during this time, and his fame brought him into contact with other renowned scientists and mathematicians.

Contributions to Mathematics

While he is most famous for inventing the barometer, Torricelli's contributions to mathematics alone earned him a place in scien-

How a Thermometer Works

Whether used to measure body temperature or the temperature of one's backyard, bulb thermometers, instruments that measure the rise or fall of temperature, typically work by the same principles. Bulb thermometers generally consist of a glass tube containing a liquid, usually mercury. Because the volume of a liquid is dependent on its temperature, the liquid within the tube will rise and fall with changes in temperature. Just as gases expand as they are heated, so do liquids; as they cool, they occupy less space. A narrow tube accentuates these changes, so a small change in temperature registers as a visible increase in the volume of the liquid. Because the bulb at the bottom of the tube is small, less than one-tenth of an inch (2.5 mm) in diameter, a change in the external temperature is readily transferred to the liquid contents of the thermometer. Mercury is often used as the liquid because it has extreme freezing (−38°F or −39°C) and boiling temperatures (674°F or 357°C) and expands at a rate that is more constant than alcohol-water mixtures.

tific history. He was primarily a geometer but was able to success-fully relate geometry and calculus to each other. His only work to be published during his lifetime, *Opera geometrica*, was published in 1644, financed by the grand duke. Other contributions were communicated through personal correspondence, from his research notes, and by compilations of his lectures on physics. *Opera geometrica* demonstrated his exceptional ability at merging classical Greek geometry and the Italian Francesco Bonaventura Cavalieri's newly developed geometry of indivisibles. Indivisibles refer to infinitesimally thin rectangles that Cavalieri used to com-pute areas underneath a curve. Torricelli extended Cavalieri's work to curved indivisibles. He also figured out calculations for

The temperature scales used most often are called Fahrenheit and Celsius. The German physicist Daniel Gabriel Fahrenheit (1686–1736) invented the first accurate thermometer in 1724 and devised the first pre-cise temperature scale. He used a scale in which the freezing and boiling points were separated by 180°, since 180 was divisible by one and 16 other whole numbers. As the lowest point on his scale, 0°F, Fahrenheit used the coldest temperature that then could be created in the laborato-ry by mixing ice with different salts. This meant that the normal freezing point of water was higher than zero; specifically, it was 32°F. After seal-ing a glass tube with mercury, Fahrenheit calibrated it by inserting it into freezing water and marking the mercury level on the glass tube "32." He labeled the level to which the mercury rose when inserted into boiling water "212°" and evenly marked 180 units between the two. (His origi-nal numbers differed slightly, but the basic method that he used remains the same.) Swedish astronomer Anders Celsius (1701–44) used a 100-point scale and assigned the freezing and boiling points of water as the constants at either end. He originally declared 100°C to be the freezing point and 0°C to be the boiling point, but his scale was later reversed. Because atmospheric pressure also affects the physical properties of a liq-uid, a constant pressure of one atmosphere is usually specified.

the geometry of a cycloid, including its area, quadrature, and tangent. A cycloid is the curve created by following a point on the circumference of a rotating circle. Interestingly, a French mathematician, Gilles Personne de Roberval, had worked out the calculations for cycloid geometry at the same time as Torricelli, but he never published his results and then accused Torricelli of stealing his work. Torricelli and Roberval furiously wrote back and forth over this issue, and at the time of his death, Torricelli was preparing to publish this correspondence.

Opera geometrica also explained projectile motion and other geometrical figures, including solids, parabolas, ellipses, and spirals. He examined parabolic trajectories initially discussed by Galileo and included experiments on the movement of water. He described the motion of liquids flowing out of an opening at the bottom of a vessel. Now known as Torricelli's theorem, he concluded that the speed of a liquid flowing from the opening in the bottom of a container is equal to the speed that a single drop of the liquid would have had when falling vertically in a vacuum from a distance equal to the top of the liquid to the point of the hole. He also proved that if a hole is made in the wall of the container, the liquid will flow out in a parabolic shape. Another principle outlined in *Opera geometrica* states that a rigid system of a number of bodies can move spontaneously on the Earth's surface only if its center of gravity descends. Though only briefly highlighted here, this entire treatise earned Torricelli the respect and admiration of mathematicians and physicists from all over Europe.

Torricelli made several other important scientific contributions. He was skilled in grinding telescope lenses, and he even earned income by making lenses by special request. He kept his methods secret until his death. Basically, he used quality materials and accurate machining of the surfaces and did not fasten the lenses with pitch or fire. Some historians believe Torricelli was responsible for turning Galileo's air thermoscope into a more accurate liquid thermometer. Torricelli argued that wind is not the evaporating exhalations of vapors from a damp earth, as had been thought at the time, but is due to changes in temperature. Cold air is denser and therefore weighs more than warm air.

Heavy, cold air naturally diffuses to areas where air is warmer and lighter in an effort to reach an equilibrium state. That is, wind forms by the air flowing from an area of greater pressure to an area of lower pressure. The greater the difference in pressure, the stronger the wind.

A Premature Ending

In October 1647, Evangelista Torricelli suddenly became gravely ill with what was probably typhoid fever. After a few days, he died at the early age of 39 and was buried in the Church of San Lorenzo in Florence. Torricelli accomplished so much in his short life. He made significant contributions to the field of geometry that helped lead to the development of integral calculus, he was the first person to create a sustained vacuum, and he invented the mercury barometer. The Austrian physicist Ernst Mach referred to him as the founder of *hydrodynamics*. Who knows what he might have accomplished had he lived twice as long.

CHRONOLOGY

1608	Evangelista Torricelli is born on October 15 in Faenza, Romagna (now Italy)
1624	Attends a Jesuit school in Faenza
1626	Becomes secretary to Benedetto Castelli
1632	Introduces himself by a letter to Galileo
1641	Becomes an assistant to Galileo
1642	Succeeds Galileo as mathematician to the grand duke of Tuscany
1643	Invents mercury barometer
1644	Publishes *Opera geometrica*
1646	Starts writing a book on cycloids
1647	Dies on October 25 in Florence, Tuscany

FURTHER READING

Allaby, Michael. *Encyclopedia of Weather and Climate*. Vol. 2. New York: Facts On File, 2002. Summarizes the knowledge of the fields of meteorology and climatology, including brief biographies of individuals who have contributed to the fields. Written in two volumes at a level appropriate for an amateur audience.

Franceschetti, Donald R., ed. *Biographical Encyclopedia of Mathematicians*. Vol. 2. New York: Marshall Cavendish, 1999. Contains brief biographies including timelines of significant events.

Gillispie, Charles C., ed. *Dictionary of Scientific Biography*. Vol. 13. New York: Scribner, 1970–76. Good source for facts concerning personal background and scientific accomplishments but assumes reader has basic knowledge of science.

Magill, Frank N., ed. *Dictionary of World Biography*. Vol. 4. Pasadena, Calif.: Salem Press, 1999. Biographies of important historical figures.

Simonis, Doris A. ed. *Lives and Legacies: Scientists, Mathematicians, and Inventors*. Phoenix, Ariz.: Oryx Press, 1999. Contains one-page profiles.

Benjamin Franklin

(1706–1790)

Benjamin Franklin is most famous for demonstrating that lightning is an electrical phenomenon. (*Library of Congress, Prints and Photographs Division [LC-USZ62-90398]*)

Lightning As an Electrical Phenomenon

Though Benjamin Franklin earned his revered position in history by helping to establish the new nation of the United States of America, he was also an accomplished scientist. He studied everything from ocean *currents* to *convection* and from electricity to whirlwinds. This famous, versatile American grew up impoverished and earned an international reputation by the time he was 40 years old.

When he demonstrated that *lightning* was an electrical phenomenon, Franklin transformed a fear-inspiring act of God into a scientifically explained act of nature.

The Family Business

Born on January 17, 1706, Benjamin Franklin was the 15th of 17 children and the youngest son born to Josiah Franklin and Abiah Folger. They lived meagerly in Boston, Massachusetts, where Josiah earned a living as a candle and soap maker. Ben began reading at an early age, and he learned things quickly. His father planned to devote Ben to church service, which required extensive schooling. Even though Ben performed outstandingly, the cost was too prohibitive, so after one year his father transferred him to another school to learn basic arithmetic and reading.

At age 10, Ben's father took him into the family business. Ben worked hard, six days a week, 12 hours each day. He cut wicks for candles, filled dipping molds, and did odd errands for his father. It was hot, and the odor inside the shop was unpleasant. Ben was interested in the sea, and his father feared that Ben might one day take off and become a sailor, as did one of his older brothers. So his father made an effort to expose him to a variety of possible careers.

Though he was an avid reader, Ben also enjoyed playing. He was an excellent swimmer and boatman. He was also a creative problem solver. One day when he was fishing with his friends, the ground where they stood became a muddy mess. Ben suggested they build a wharf to fish from using a bundle of rocks from a nearby construction site. After dinner they proceeded to complete the task. Unfortunately, they were caught the next day and had to return the rocks to the rightful owner. When Ben tried to defend himself against too harsh a punishment from his father, his father told him that nothing was useful if not honest. This was a valuable lesson for young Ben, so much so that he recorded the event in his autobiography decades later. He credited his father with often being sought after for advice on personal and business matters from neighbors and fellow church members. Ben exhibited this same quality as an adult.

Printing Apprentice

By the time he was 12 years old, Ben's interest in books led him to the decision to become a printer. Coincidentally, Ben's older brother James was a printer. Ben signed an apprentice agreement with him, indenturing himself until the age of 21. In return, Ben would earn room and board, the skills of the trade, and during the last year, he would also earn wages. Ben learned the trade quickly and took advantage of having access to so many books, often staying up late at night to finish a book so he could return it by morning. One customer gave Ben access to his personal library. During these years, he taught himself arithmetic, a subject with which he had struggled years before. He also became interested in poetry, a hobby his father encouraged him to drop since there was no money to be made in it.

In 1721, James started what was only the second newspaper in New England, the *New England Courant*. Occasionally his friends submitted articles that James would publish. Ben enjoyed writing as well as reading, and one day he anonymously submitted an article for publication under the created personality of Silence Dogood, a chatty, opinionated widow. James and his friends thought the article was worthy of publication, and Ben continued to anonymously submit 14 more articles. When he tired of the game and confessed to his brother, James was angry with him for his trickery. This incident worsened already bad relations between the two Franklins. Ben felt his brother treated him more like a slave than an apprentice. When James was imprisoned for one month for publishing an offensive article, Ben managed the paper. A few months later James was forbidden to publish his paper, so he transferred the paper to Ben's name. Feelings were still bad, however, and when Ben told his brother he wanted out of the arrangement, James threatened to tell all the nearby printers to not hire him. Ben worked up a plan to run away to New York, thinking surely he could find employment there. To gain secret passage onto a boat so his brother would not find out about his sneaking away, Ben's friend contrived a story that Ben had gotten a girl pregnant and was fleeing to escape having to marry the girl. Apparently, the ship's captain thought this was a good excuse to keep silent about things and took him aboard.

On His Own

Franklin arrived in New York at the age of 17 only to find himself unable to get a job. The printer there mentioned that he thought his son in Philadelphia was looking for someone to help in his printing business. Franklin set out immediately, but without funds or prior planning, it took him several days to arrive. When he did, he found out the son had already hired someone. Franklin was not too discouraged though. There were two printers in Philadelphia, and the second one, Samuel Keimer, was impressed by Franklin's demonstrated abilities. He hired him and set up rooming for Franklin with Mr. Read next door. While under Keimer's employ, Franklin came to the attention of the governor of Pennsylvania, William Keith. Keith was so impressed by Franklin he suggested that he set up his own printing business.

Franklin went back home to Boston with a recommendation letter from Governor Keith asking his father for support. His family had not heard at all from Franklin for over seven months. Though Franklin's family was thrilled to see the runaway, his father refused the request to help Franklin establish his own business. He thought Franklin was too young and inexperienced. Keith disagreed and promised to financially support Franklin. He sent him to London to purchase the necessary types and presses. Unfortunately, the pledged credit letter from Governor Keith on which Franklin counted in order to make his purchases never arrived in London. It is likely that Keith had no credit to offer anyhow. Consequently, Franklin was stuck in London without funds for a return voyage.

During the next one and one-half years, Franklin worked for two different printing houses in London. He made acquaintances and enjoyed the culture. Since his father had emigrated from England, Franklin felt this was his motherland. One person he met, Thomas Denham, was planning to open a store in Philadelphia and extended an offer to Franklin to assist in its running. Franklin helped Denham gather necessary goods, and in 1726, they traveled back to America together. Things seemed marvelous, but in February 1727, both men fell ill. Denham did not recover, and now at age 21, Franklin once again found himself in a city with no relation and no job. He tucked his tail between his legs and asked Keimer for a job.

Franklin was humbled, but Keimer was quite pleased to have such able hands in his employ once more. Several new apprentices and assistants worked in his shop now, and Keimer wanted Franklin to teach them everything he knew. Franklin did such a great job teaching Keimer's employees that after a while Keimer decided he did not really need Franklin anymore. He notified Franklin that he was lowering his wages, and soon after, Franklin angrily left to open a business with Hugh Meredith, one of Keimer's assistants. Funded by the credit of Meredith's father, the business was running satisfactorily, but Meredith was not as interested in the necessary hard work as Franklin, and it turned out that his father could not pay the debts. Franklin borrowed money from friends to buy out the business in 1730.

Around this time, Franklin started a club called the Junto. The members wrote essays and discussed matters ranging from political to moral to scientific. In his personal life, Franklin began courting Miss Deborah Read, the daughter of his former landlord. They had dated and even became informally engaged before Franklin took off for London in 1724. They married in 1730. Interestingly, they had several inconveniences to overcome before being legally married. Franklin had an illegitimate toddler son. Deborah had been previously married but not divorced, and the whereabouts of her husband were unknown. Franklin and Deborah eventually had two children of their own, Francis (who died at age four from smallpox) and Sally.

Poor Richard's Almanack

Franklin wanted to start a newspaper, but Keimer heard about this and beat him to it by starting the *Pennsylvania Gazette*. Franklin started writing articles for the competitor's paper, contributing to Keimer's failure. Franklin bought the paper from Keimer and made it a success. For the next several decades he used this paper to advance many social and political causes he supported. In 1732, Franklin started publishing *Poor Richard's Almanack*. Almanacs were very popular in the 18th century. Authors annually compiled data concerning weather, tides, and other practical information. Franklin included original and borrowed bits of wisdom such as

"Early to bed, early to rise, makes a man healthy, wealthy, and wise." His *Almanack* was a best seller until he stopped publishing it in 1758.

By earning a reputation of being a hard, honest worker, Franklin obtained much of the government's official printing business, including printing paper money. He was instrumental in initiating many public institutions in Philadelphia. For example, he started the first public library by soliciting subscriptions for fees that were used to purchase books to which subscribers shared access. He also started the Union Fire Company of Philadelphia (1736), beefed up the city's police force, got the city's main streets paved to prevent mud from being tracked into the local businesses, headed a campaign to open the first hospital in Philadelphia (1752), and founded the first college there (now the University of Pennsylvania). While accomplishing all this, he also served as postmaster of Philadelphia (1737–53) and then deputy postmaster general for all the colonies (1753–74), and he organized a voluntary military defense unit (1755). He served as clerk of the Pennsylvania assembly from 1736 until 1751, when he was elected a member. He made several trips overseas serving in this capacity, not only as the Pennsylvania assembly representative, but later also for New Jersey, Georgia, and Massachusetts. The details of these numerous accomplishments have filled hundreds of volumes of texts and history books.

The Pennsylvania Fireplace

In 1748, Franklin retired from his printing business and began thinking about scientific matters. In the mid-1740s, he founded the American Philosophical Society to "promote useful knowledge in the sciences and humanities." The members shared knowledge on plants, animals, and geography and published scientific reports. This was the first enduring scientific organization in the New World, and it still exists today.

Around 1740, Franklin invented what he called the Pennsylvania fireplace, more commonly known as the Franklin stove. Fireplaces then were very inefficient as they required masses of wood, which had to be chopped and collected often from great distances. Once burning, most of the heat was drawn out of the room and up the chimney. In order to get warmth from a fireplace, one had to basically sit right in front of the fire, thus if there were many people in a room, only a few could enjoy the warmth of the fire. Though Franklin only had two years of formal schooling as a child, he was able to solve problems in a very methodical fashion. He considered the main problems of the traditional fireplace to be that most of the hot air immediately went up and out of the chimney and that in the process a vacuum was created in the room, drawing cold air from any cracks in the doorway or windows, creating a draft. He designed a more efficient convection fireplace that took advantage of the conductivity of metal and the fact that warm air naturally rises.

In the Pennsylvania fireplace, fresh air is drawn in below the fireplace and rises up within a hollow chamber behind the actual fire. The same walls that direct the hot, smoky air from the burning wood to the chamber's top plate, which acts like a radiator, enclose the chamber. The heat from the walls is transferred to the fresh air as it rises in the air chamber behind the fire, and the newly warmed air leaves the air box through holes in the sides of the fireplace and enters the room. Meanwhile, the smoky air continues to travel down the wall on the back of the air chamber and then up through the chimney. American people have been warmed by this invention for more than 200 years. Franklin never applied for a patent.

In October 1743, Franklin was anxious to view an anticipated lunar eclipse, but a storm in Philadelphia prevented him from being able to observe it. After reading the Boston newspaper, he learned that Bostonians had a clear view of the eclipse, but the next day they had been hit

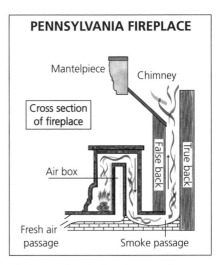

The Pennsylvania fireplace used convection heating to warm a room more efficiently than an ordinary fireplace. After being heated in a compartment behind the fireplace, warm air entered the room through a hole in the side of the air box.

with a severe storm. Though at the time people believed that storms started and stopped in the same location, Franklin suspected the storm in Philadelphia and Boston was the same storm. He began checking weather reports from all over the east coast and realized that not only were storms mobile, but they also typically moved toward the northeast up the Atlantic coast. He had discovered what is now referred to as the "northeaster." He also noted that though the general direction of a storm moved in one direction, the comprising winds came from several directions. This allowed him to theorize about the effect of different atmospheric pressures in moving storms.

Experiments with Electricity

Beginning in the 1740s, Franklin started experimenting with electricity in his home. He wrote reports of most of his observations and sent them to a fellow scientist, Peter Collinson, in London. These works were collected and eventually published in 1751 as *Experiments and Observations on Electricity*. He coined several terms including *charge* and *battery* as well as *plus* and *minus* to describe opposite electrical charges. One of his early discoveries was that a pointed *conductor* drew charge from a greater distance than a blunt one. He helped scientists understand electrical charge was not something that one created but something that one collected from nature. He also introduced the law of conservation of charge, which stated that the amount of electric charge produced in any process is zero. In 1753, the Royal Society of London awarded Franklin the Copley Medal for his advances in the field of electricity. He was elected a fellow in 1756.

Franklin was one of the first to experiment with how a *Leyden jar* worked. A Leyden jar was essentially a glass jar coated with metal foil on the inside and outside, filled with water, and plugged with a cork. A metal rod or chain extended from the outside of the jar, through the cork, to the water on the interior. Such a device was used to store collected electricity. When the outside foil was *grounded* (by someone holding it) and the outside and inside were connected through a conductor, the electricity was discharged as a spark. For entertainment purposes, a person would act as the conductor for these gadgets by touching the rod. Franklin was curious how they worked. He found that the outside and inside conductors were oppositely but equally charged. When he dumped the water from a charged Leyden jar into another glass bottle, no charge remained in the water. When he refilled the emptied jar with unelectrified water, a spark could still be produced. This showed that it was the glass itself that produced the shock. To further demonstrate that the glass had been charged, he covered a glass windowpane with lead sheets on both sides. He charged the lead and then removed the sheets one at a time. Neither sheet was charged upon removal, but the glass was. Today we call such a device a *capacitor* or *condenser.* A capacitor is a device that stores electrical energy, as did the glass windowpane, and consists of two parallel conducting materials held close to one another but not touching. Capacitors are used in all sorts of electrical circuits, including radios and televisions.

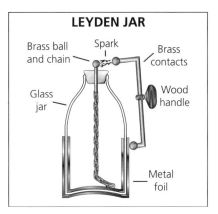

Leyden jars were used to collect and store static electricity.

Franklin pondered the similarities between lightning and electricity. Both produced light, traveled in a crooked path, and made a cracking sound. To test whether lightning was indeed an electrical phenomenon, he planned to have a long metal rod erected atop a tall local church steeple and hoped to collect an electrical charge from lightning. While waiting for the rod to be installed, however, another man copied his idea and was able to collect a charge from lightning. Meanwhile, in 1752, Franklin came up with another way to test whether lightning was electrical. He built a kite from a silk handkerchief stretched over two overlapping wooden rods and attached a pointed wire to the end of one of the rods. At the end of the kite string, Franklin tied a silk ribbon and a metal key. If electricity was present in the sky, he would be able to draw the static charge down the wet string and into the key. He was careful to stand under a dry shelter so the silk ribbon he was holding would not get wet. After waiting for a while with his son William, Franklin

So What Actually Happened?

Electricity is a form of energy that occurs when charges are present in matter. The atoms that comprise matter contain positively charged protons in their nuclei and negatively charged electrons orbiting their exterior. Conductors are substances such as metals with electrons that are loosely bound and therefore able to move about freely within the material. Because opposite charges attract, if a positively charged substance is held to the conductor, the negatively charged electrons will move toward the positively charged object. This motion of electrons creates a *current,* or a flowing of charges, until a nonconducting material is reached. Nonconductors are materials such as dry wood or rubber in which the electrons are held very close to the atomic nuclei. Because of this, they act as good *insulators.* The Earth contains enormous amounts of both positive and negative charges and thus, a current is said to be "grounded" if a con-

noticed that frayed bits of thread along the string were standing straight up. As he approached the key with his knuckle, a spark shot out from the key toward his hand. Incidentally, two other men died trying to replicate this sort of experiment because they did not properly ground the charge, and they were struck by the lightning.

Lightning is very dangerous. If a person is struck, the victim can die or suffer serious consequences. If a building is struck, it can suffer serious damage or catch on fire. For protection, Franklin invented the *lightning rod,* figuring that a good conductor could draw the electrical charges out of the sky and safely direct them away from the house itself into the ground. People started attaching tall metal rods to buildings. They reached from six (1.8 m) to eight feet (2.4 m) over the top of the building they were meant to protect and extended down into the ground, drawing the electrical fire out of the clouds and carrying the current away where no damage would result.

ductor leads to the Earth, delivering the flowing electrons to it. *Static electricity* is caused by friction, like the friction that results from shuffling feet along the carpet. The friction separates the charges, but they remain at rest. There is no flow of electrons from one object to another as in a current.

During a storm, tiny ice particles inside the clouds rub and knock against each other. In doing so, a charge builds up inside the clouds; the negatively charged side usually faces the ground. The Earth's positive charges build up around objects that protrude from the ground, such as tall trees or even people. If a cloud comes near enough to one of these conductors, the charge flows through the object toward the Earth, where it dissipates. When the negatively charged particles are transferred from the clouds to a good conductor, a flash of light is given off—the lightning. The heat from this reaction, which is about twice as hot as the surface of the Sun, causes a rapid expansion of the surrounding air, giving us thunder. Since light travels faster than sound, the flash of lightning is seen before the thunder is heard. The difference in the time between the lightning flash and the sound of thunder is indicative of the distance between the observer and the actual event.

Studies on Whirlwinds and the Gulf Stream

Interested in other weather-related phenomenon, Franklin was known to have chased whirlwinds. In 1755, he wrote a description of one to Collinson. This was the first detailed description of the miniature tornadoes. He followed one and was able to observe its motion by the dirt and leaves it picked up. He noted that while the spinning motion was very rapid, the motion forward was slow ("as a man on foot"). The whirlwind did not move in a straight line, the speed was inconsistent, and its direction was opposite that of the general wind. Franklin recorded its height and diameter as it moved and grew. He also tried to break the whirlwind by striking it with a whip, but this had no effect. He correctly speculated that the center contained a vacuum.

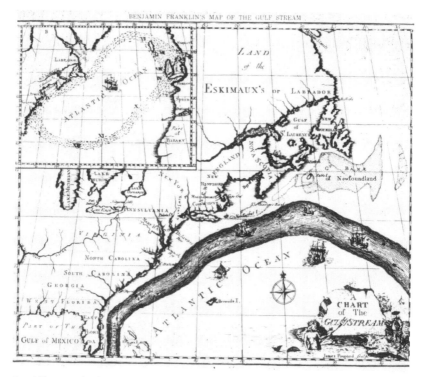

Franklin was the first to create a map of the Gulf Stream current. *(Courtesy of NOAA Central Library)*

Always the scientist, in his eight crossings of the Atlantic, Franklin kept careful records regarding weather patterns, temperatures, and atmospheric and oceanic circulation. Ocean travel was very important in the 18th century. Traveling from Boston to New York was faster by water than by land. Many items, such as precious books and equipment, could only be purchased overseas, but Atlantic crossings took between six and eight weeks and were dangerous. Franklin's older brother Josiah died when his ship went down at sea. Since Franklin was serving as postmaster general, he was aware of complaints that packages took two weeks longer to arrive in New England from England than vice versa. He remembered noticing as a young man traveling across the Atlantic, that mid-voyage the water's color lightened, there was more seaweed floating in the water, and the winds became warmer, usually signs that one was near land. However, after a few days the water turned dark again, the seaweed disappeared, and the winds cooled. He talked to his cousin, a Nantucket sea captain familiar with the area. From his investigations into this matter, he produced the first-known chart of the *Gulf Stream*, a major surface current that travels up the eastern coast of America and across the north Atlantic to northwestern Europe. The Gulf Stream affects weather patterns along its route. Even on his last voyage in 1785, Franklin continued to collect data to refine this chart. He developed a special device for measuring temperatures 100 feet (30 m) below the surface of the water. Because of the Gulf Stream's effect on marine life, a detailed chart was useful not only for travelers, but also for whalers and fishermen. The Gulf Stream continues to be used today in weather forecasting.

A Founder of a New Nation

Toward the end of his life, Franklin kept busy with the details of founding a new nation, the United States of America. Though initially Franklin believed America was better off remaining under British rule, over time he came to passionately support her independence. He journeyed to England several times, initially to represent the rights of the colonists who had no official representation in Parliament and later to negotiate a peace treaty with England. While he was there for one extended period (from 1764 to 1775) protesting taxes the British imposed on American imports, his wife passed away. Representing the colonies was a violent struggle at times; Franklin alternately assumed the role of villain and hero. He returned home to America for good in 1785.

Within a week of arriving back in Philadelphia in fall 1785, Franklin was named a delegate to the Constitutional Convention. The delegates' charge was to draft a document that formulated the laws upon which the new nation would thrive. Though Franklin now suffered from common ailments of old age and had to be carried the few blocks down the street by a group of convicts, his presence at the meetings was influential. His wisdom and humor were instrumental in unifying the thirteen colonies into one nation. Franklin was the only person to sign all four documents that were instrumental in forming the United States of America: the

Declaration of Independence, the Treaty of Alliance with France, the Peace Treaty with England, and the Constitution of the United States of America.

During the last years of his life, Franklin suffered from kidney stones and became bedridden. The man who tamed lightning died peacefully at the age of 84, on April 17, 1790. He was buried with his youngest son, Francis, and wife Deborah in Philadelphia. Franklin was the first American to achieve international recognition as a scientist. His research was pivotal in the maturation of electricity into a new field of science and the invention of the language to describe it. Though self-educated, he was awarded several honorary degrees during his lifetime. He is remembered as a respected meteorologist, oceanographer, physicist, philosopher, writer, public servant, and statesman. Besides the Franklin stove and the lightning rod, Franklin invented bifocal lenses, a musical instrument called the armonica, a rocking chair with a built-in fan, a chair with a writing table, and other things. He also conceived of daylight savings time. He never applied for patents on any of his inventions, and today society continues to benefit from his creativity and generosity.

CHRONOLOGY

1706	Benjamin Franklin is born on January 17 in Boston, Massachusetts
1718	Begins serving as a printing apprentice to older brother
1722	Writes Silence Dogood essays
1723	Moves to Philadelphia and works as a printer
1724-26	Works as a printer in London
1728	Opens own printing business with Hugh Meredith
1729	Purchases the *Pennsylvania Gazette*
1732-58	Publishes *Poor Richard's Almanack*
1736	Founds the Union Fire Company
1736-51	Serves as clerk of the Pennsylvania assembly

1737	Is appointed postmaster of Philadelphia
1742-44	Founds the University of Pennsylvania and invents the Pennsylvania fireplace
1751	Publishes work on electricity, founds the Pennsylvania Hospital, and is elected to the Pennsylvania assembly
1752	Performs kite experiment with son William and invents lightning rod
1753-74	Serves as joint deputy postmaster general for North America
1757-62	Travels to England to represent the Pennsylvania assembly
1764-75	Travels to London again
1775	Is elected to the Continental Congress
1776	Signs the Declaration of Independence
1778	Signs the treaty of alliance with France
1781-83	Negotiates a peace treaty with Britain
1785	Returns to Philadelphia, becomes a delegate to the Constitutional Convention, and publishes a chart of the Gulf Stream
1787	Signs the Constitution of the United States of America
1790	Dies at home on April 17 in Philadelphia, at age 84

FURTHER READING

Adler, David A. *B. Franklin, Printer.* New York: Holiday House, 2001. Follows the life of the accomplished American who achieved greatness as a writer, scientist, inventor, and statesman. Intended for juvenile readers.

Brands, H. W. *The First American: The Life and Times of Benjamin Franklin.* New York: Doubleday, 2000. Vivid and thorough account of Franklin's life and the many roles he played.

The Electric Ben Franklin. Independence Hall Association. Available online. URL: http://www.ushistory.org/franklin. Accessed on

February 8, 2005. Very useful Web site with many links including links to Franklin's complete autobiography, the kite experiment, and special articles about Franklin.

Garraty, John A., and Mark C. Carnes, eds. *American National Biography.* Vol. 8. New York: Oxford University Press, 1999. Brief account of lives and works of famous Americans in encyclopedia format.

Looby, Chris. *Benjamin Franklin.* New York: Chelsea House, 1990. Summarizes Franklin's contributions as a statesman, inventor, philanthropist, publisher, and revolutionary. Written for a juvenile audience.

Roop, Peter, and Connie Roop. *Benjamin Franklin.* New York: Scholastic, 2000. A biography of the noted statesman and inventor. Includes excerpts from his letters and works.

Shaw, Peter, ed. *The Autobiography and Other Writings by Benjamin Franklin.* New York: Bantam Books, 1982. Contains selections from Franklin's newspaper articles, *Poor Richard's Almanack*, correspondence, essays, and his autobiography.

Luke Howard

(1772–1864)

Luke Howard proposed a system of classifying cloud formations. *(Reproduced with permission of the Royal Meteorological Society)*

Classification of Cloud Types

Since the earliest of times, humans have appreciated the beauty of the heavens. The act of lying in thick, green grass on a hillside among spring daisies on a sunny afternoon could be further enhanced only by something as awe-inspiring as the view of several white, fluffy clouds in a variety of shapes gently floating through the blue sky. How peaceful. What about the breathtaking scenery from the window of an airplane ascending over a mountain range covered with an expanse of wispy fragments of clouds? No wonder the image of clouds has been adapted into many of our everyday expressions. Someone who has his or her "head in the clouds" is in a faraway, dreamy state. Being on "cloud nine" describes an elated, emotional condition. The word "cloud" can also conjure up negative or dark emotions, hinting at obscurity or gloominess. Choosing the correct words to describe something so precisely is an art, one appreciated by the Englishman who took upon himself the task of naming the different types of clouds. Luke Howard was a chemist by training but was considered an expert meteorologist of his time. By classifying and naming the clouds, he invented a language that launched an entire new branch of science.

Watching the Sky

Luke Howard was the first of five children born to Robert Howard and his second wife, Elizabeth Leatham, on November 28, 1772. Robert already had three sons from his first wife, who had died of consumption (now called tuberculosis). Robert owned a tin and iron workshop, and his children often helped out at work. The business was successful, and the family was able to send Luke to a private school in Burford, near Oxford, England. He began there when he was eight and attended the academy for seven years. Hillside Academy was run by a strict schoolmaster, and there was not much time for playing, but in between Latin class and studying, Luke found time to gaze in amazement at the heavens.

When Luke was 10 years old, a remarkable series of events led to bizarre weather patterns and unusual sights in the sky. A relentless fog settled over the Northern Hemisphere after tremendous volcanic eruptions in both Iceland and Japan. The fog (later referred to as the "Great Fogg") was persistent and caused unpleasant heat, symptoms of illness in people, and insect infestations. That same year a bright meteor passed through the skies of western Europe causing a spectacular light show that left a lasting impression on young Luke.

Science in His Spare Time

After leaving school in 1788, Luke returned home. He spent time working in his parents' garden, where he set up a miniature meteorological station. He used a rain gauge, thermometer, and barometer to record weather observations twice daily. Though he was quite content, after a few weeks his father sent Luke to Stockport in Cheshire to serve as an apprentice to a retail chemist, Ollive Sims. Sims was an acquaintance of Robert's and also an orthodox Quaker. Free time seemed an extravagance during the next six years of Luke's life. He did not enjoy the work and missed science terribly. In the little spare time he found, he managed to teach himself much about botany and chemistry.

Luke returned home to London in 1794 and worked a few months for a wholesale druggist, but he still did not enjoy the work of a chemist. He persuaded his father to lend him enough money to start his own pharmacy business and moved into a tiny area above his shop. While the labor was the same, being his own boss allowed Luke to manage his hours, and he started attending chemistry lectures twice a week. He made friends with other young men in situations similar to his own—men who enjoyed science but had to earn a living by some alternate lackluster means. Most were dissenters like Luke, meaning they did not belong to the Church of England and therefore could not attend public grammar schools or English universities.

William Allen was a fellow pharmacist who became good friends with Luke. Allen worked for a commercial pharmacy and took over when the current director retired. The company was renamed Allen and Hanbury's and was eventually taken over by Glaxo Wellcome (today GlaxoSmithKline). Allen became the director for a new manufacturing laboratory at Plaistow in Essex and asked Luke to be his manager. Luke had married Mariabella Eliot in December 1796, and she was pregnant with their first child. In need of a more secure job, he and his bride moved out of London. Howard earned his living as a chemist but devoted himself to studying science in his leisure time.

On the Modification of Clouds

Around the same time, Allen founded the Askesian Society, a forum for discussions about the natural sciences. Howard presented his first paper, "Average Barometer," to this society in 1800. In early 1802, he presented another paper, "Theories of Rain." During the winter of 1802–03, Howard presented the lecture that gave him the most recognition, "On the Modification of Clouds."

At the time, meteorology had not yet been established as a science. Though attempts had been made to create a language to describe the skies, natural philosophers and others who were interested in *nephology* (the study of clouds) shared no universally accepted vocabulary. Part of the reason was due to the inherent difficulty in attempting to classify something that is constantly changing. Furthermore, people thought that there were too many different kinds of clouds to try to name them. In addition to cloud color, usually white or various shades of gray, observers of the sky used vague descriptive words such as hazy, fleecy, or streaky and compared cloud shapes to castles or mare's tails. Howard deliberately set out to change all that.

The system he proposed in his Askesian Society lecture was so simple that it seemed blatantly obvious. He suggested that though there were an infinite number of cloud shapes, the number of distinct forms was limited to a distinct few. He also stated that the shapes and forms of clouds were predictable, as their formation was a natural, physical process dependent upon physical characteristics such as temperature, humidity, and air pressure. Inspired by Carl Linnaeus's binomial nomenclature system of the living world using the Latin language, Howard declared that there were three main types of clouds: *cirrus* (meaning curl of hair), *cumulus* (meaning heap), and *stratus* (meaning layer). Four other types were modifications of the three basic families: cirro-cumulus, cirro-stratus, cumulo-stratus, and cumulo-cirro-stratus or *nimbus*. He called these types "modifications" because clouds are constantly morphing; today such categories are called classifications. Howard also presented watercolors of his own creation to illustrate each category. Howard's seven modifications are briefly described below.

1. Cirrus: the least dense, occurring at the highest altitudes and having a wispy, threadlike appearance
2. Cumulus: the densest, formed at lower altitudes from a horizontal base, and growing upward in spherical heaps
3. Stratus: the lowest clouds, extending in horizontal sheets

PROPERTY OF FISCHER MIDDLE SCHOOL
1305 LONG GROVE DRIVE
AURORA, IL 60504

4. Cirro-cumulus: formed by fibrous cirrus clouds collapsing downward into spherical masses
5. Cirro-stratus: formed by fibrous cirrus clouds extending horizontally
6. Cumulo-stratus: dense, mushroom-shaped clouds formed from cumulus prior to the onset of rain
7. Cumulo-cirro-stratus or nimbus: rain cloud

The reaction of the audience to Howard's "On the Modification of Clouds" seminar was animated. They immediately recognized the significance of Howard's presentation and knew they had witnessed a historical scientific event. One member of the audience that night was Askesian Society member Alexander Tilloch, founder of the *Philosophical Magazine*, a widely read science journal popular among the general public as well as budding scientists. Tilloch requested that Howard submit his essay. Howard added sections, including one on *dew* formation and another on the formation of precipitation, and in April 1803, the final 15,000-word essay was published. Knowledge of Howard's cloud classification system quickly spread around the

Cirrus clouds are high-level, white clouds that develop in filaments or patches. *(Courtesy of the National Oceanic and Atmospheric Administration/ Department of Commerce)*

Cloud Formation

Clouds are loosely formed collections of hundreds of millions of droplets of condensed moisture at altitudes high above the Earth's surface. Clouds generally contain droplets of liquid water if above 32°F (0°C) or ice crystals if below 32°F (0°C), though cloud droplets sometimes are supercooled, meaning they can exist in the liquid form at temperatures approaching −40°F (−40°C). Within the *troposphere*, which extends from the Earth's surface six miles (9.7 km) upward, the air pressure and temperature decrease as altitude increases. Water from the Earth's surface evaporates and rises. As it rises, it cools. It finally condenses onto particulate matter, such as dust in the air, when it reaches its *dew point* or *frost point*, the temperature at which the air becomes saturated and transforms the vapor into a liquid or solid, respectively. The more moisture air contains, the lower the temperature at which it condenses.

The shape assumed by a cloud is a result of the method by which it was formed. This has a lot to do with the manner by which the air reached the higher altitude where it condensed. Air rises by several methods. Convection is a process by which warm air naturally rises because it is lighter, or less dense, than cooler air. So as the ground

world. Interestingly, the French naturalist Jean-Baptiste Lamarck had proposed a cloud classification scheme earlier that year based on appearance, but it had gone largely unrecognized.

Howard continued studying meteorological phenomena and spoke and wrote prolifically on the subject. In 1806, Howard began regularly publishing his "Meteorological Register" in *The Athenaeum: A Magazine of Literary and Miscellaneous Information*. In a seven-lecture series given in Tottenham in 1817, he reorganized his seven modifi-

Orgographic lifting of air masses over mountain peaks is one method of cloud formation. *(Courtesy of the National Oceanic and Atmospheric Administration/ Department of Commerce)*

becomes heated by the Sun, heat is radiated up into the air. Another method by which warm air rises is called frontal lifting or convergence, which occurs when two *air masses* of different temperatures meet. When a mass of warm, moist air bumps into a mass of cooler, dry air, the warmer air moves up and over the cooler air, forming clouds in the process. Lastly, *orgographic lifting* occurs when a mass of air encounters an elevated landmass, such as a mountain, and is forced to travel up the slope of the physical barrier.

cations based on altitude. Cirrus was the highest, followed by cirro-cumulus, cirro-stratus, cumulus, cumulo-stratus, nimbus, and finally, stratus, which was simply mist or fog. He also devised a shorthand method for recording modifications: Cirrus \ ; Cumulus ∩ ; and Stratus _ . Combinations of these three symbols were used to notate all seven modifications. These *Seven Lectures in Meteorology* were compiled and published in 1837 in what became the first textbook on meteorology.

Authority on Meteorology

Another of Howard's major works was *The Climate of London* (1818–20), considered the first text on *urban meteorology*, the study of the climate and atmospheric phenomena surrounding cities. He was the first to describe the concept of *heat islands*. On warm days, urban environments can have temperatures of six to eight degrees Fahrenheit warmer than surrounding rural areas. One cause of this in cities is an increase in dark surfaces such as pavement, which absorbs heat. A decrease in vegetation, which shades and cools, also contributes. Another cause is the widespread use of fuel within the city. Urban heat islands increase the demand for air conditioning and lead to increased pollution. In *The Climate of London*, Howard discussed a unique city fog, now called *smog*, which is simply polluted fog mixed with smoke. A second edition of this popular work published in 1833 grew to three volumes.

While Howard was busy researching and writing about clouds and other meteorological topics, others were writing about him. Thomas Forster collected and published Howard's literature in a book titled *Researches about Atmospheric Phenomena* in 1813. Forster was initially a staunch supporter of Howard's cloud classification system when critics cried that the Latin language was too difficult for ordinary people to grasp. Forster even suggested several additional terms to be even more descriptive, such as *planus* to depict large continuous sheets and *floccosus* for clouds divided into loose fleeces, but his new terms never stuck. Interestingly, Forster himself later tried to cut in on Howard's system by pushing for an English translation of the classification system to be adopted. Fortunately, others were in favor of maintaining the integrity of the originally proposed system, and though Forster's translations began to be used, they never were universally accepted and eventually faded away.

Science was not the only area impacted by Howard's work. Ship captains started using his system and notation for recording weather observations at sea. An English ship commander named Sir Francis Beaufort was impressed with Howard's creativity and originality and devised a similar means for classifying winds, called the *Beaufort wind scale*. This allowed sea travelers to compare conditions more objectively than previously.

Howard and Allen amicably ended their working partnership in 1807. Howard became the sole owner of Luke Howard and Company of Stratford, a chemical manufacturing company. That same year one of his daughters died at age 18 months from whooping cough.

One of the highest honors an English scientist can receive was bestowed upon Howard in 1821. He was elected a fellow of the Royal Society of London in recognition of his advancements to the field of meteorology.

In 1823, Tilloch proposed the formation of the Meteorological Society of London, and Howard was a founding member. Forster, with whom Howard had developed a cordial relationship by now, was also a founding member. Howard gave the society's second lecture, entitled "Curious Effects of the Radiation of Heat." Unfortunately, after the society broke for the summer in 1824, the meetings did not resume that fall. Around 1824, Howard bought property in rural Yorkshire, seeking a less hectic life. He was very involved in his community. He taught voluntarily at the local Quaker school, participated in an antislavery campaign, and helped raise and distribute funds to German peasants of the Napoleonic wars. Thus he had less time to devote to meteorology. Except for the second edition of *The Climate of London*, he did not publish anything new for 20 years. The newly formed Meteorological Society of London died off without his enthusiasm and leadership and did not reform until 12 years later, but even then Howard did not take an active role. In 1850, it became the British Meteorological Society and then in 1883, the Royal Meteorological Society.

In 1852, Luke's wife Mariabella died after 56 years of marriage. Luke moved in with his eldest son in Tottenham, where he lived for the remaining 12 years of his life.

Modern Cloud Classification

The man who invented a language that birthed the field of nephology passed away on March 21, 1864. He was 91 years old. Luke Howard was buried at Winchmore Hill Burial Ground near his wife, parents, and half brothers. He has been described as a thoughtful person who was often found looking upward, into the clouds. This quiet

From an airplane above the stratocumulus, one may observe multiple layers of clouds. *(Courtesy of the National Oceanic and Atmospheric Administration/ Department of Commerce)*

man was honored not only by fellow scientists, but also by literary and artistic geniuses. The German philosopher and poet Johann Wolfgang von Goethe was so delighted by Howard's essay "On the Modification of Clouds" that he developed a correspondence with Howard to learn more about the man behind the genius. Goethe penned four poems devoted to Luke Howard and his cloud classification system and named the poetic collection *Howards Ehrengedächtnis.* Samuel Taylor Coleridge and Percy Bysshe Shelley also honored Howard in their poetry. Howard's vivid descriptions of clouds inspired more than 200 beautiful paintings by John Constable of England between 1820 and 1822. Howard's legacy is forever remembered through these literary and artistic media. The year 1896 was celebrated as the International Year of Clouds; the language of the clouds was permanently declared and the first *International Cloud Atlas* was published. In April 2002, the British Meteorological Office and English Heritage honored Howard by posting a plaque on the London home where he spent his final years.

Amazingly, the modern system of cloud classification is only a slightly updated version of Howard's original proposition. There are two basic types, *cumuliform* (the puffy, billowing clouds) and *stratiform* (the flat, layered clouds). They are further classified by altitude, as suggested by Howard in his *Seven Lectures in Meteorology.* The high clouds with bases above 20,000 feet (about 6,000 m) are cirrus (Ci), cirrocumulus (Cc), and cirrostratus (Cs). Intermediate clouds with bases between 6,500 and 20,000 feet (about 2,000–6,000 m) include altocumulus (Ac), altostratus (As), and nimbostratus (Ns). The low clouds with bases below 6,500 feet (about 2,000 m) are stratocumulus (Sc), stratus (St), and cumulus (Cu). Cumulonimbus (Cb) clouds can extend through all three bands. Howard would be pleased that his original Latin terms stuck and that the categories are clear and simple enough for even the amateur observer to confidently name what he or she sees in the firmament.

CHRONOLOGY

| 1772 | Luke Howard is born on November 28 in London, England |
| 1780–88 | Attends Quaker grammar school Hillside Academy |

1788–94	Is apprentice to retail chemist
1794	Starts own pharmacy
1796	William Allen founds Askesian Society
1796–07	Works with William Allen
1802	Reads famous paper "On the Modifications of Clouds" to the Askesian Society
1803	Publishes "On the Modifications of Clouds" in *Philosophical Magazine*
1813	Forster publishes *Researches about Atmospheric Phenomena*
1817	Howard gives seven lectures on meteorology in Tottenham. Johann Wolfgang von Goethe writes four poems in honor of Howard
1818–20	Publishes first edition of *The Climate of London*
1833	Publishes second edition of *The Climate of London*
1837	Publishes *Seven Lectures in Meteorology*, considered the first textbook on meteorology
1864	Dies on March 21 in London, at age 91
1896	International Year of Clouds

FURTHER READING

Allaby, Michael. *Encyclopedia of Weather and Climate.* Vol. 1. New York: Facts On File, 2002. Summarizes the knowledge of the fields of meteorology and climatology and includes brief biographies of individuals who have contributed to the fields. Written in two volumes at a level appropriate for an amateur audience.

Day, John A. "Luke Howard—The Godfather of Clouds." Available online. URL: http://www.cloudman.com/luke/luke_howard. htm. Last updated May 2004. Three essays summarizing Howard's background and famous lecture on cloud nomenclature.

Hamblyn, Richard. *The Invention of Clouds: How an Amateur Meteorologist Forged the Language of the Skies.* New York: Picador,

2001. Story of events leading up to and following Howard's 1802 lecture on the nomenclature to classify clouds.

Heidorn, Keith C. "Luke Howard: The Man Who Named the Clouds." Available online. URL: http://www.islandnet.com/~see/weather/history/howard.htm. Accessed February 8, 2005. Three essays summarizing Howard's background and famous lecture on cloud nomenclature.

Stephen, Leslie, and Sidney Lee, eds. *The Dictionary of National Biography.* Vol. 10. London: Oxford University Press, 1921–22. Brief account of lives and works of famous people from Great Britain in encyclopedia format.

Sir Francis Beaufort

(1774–1857)

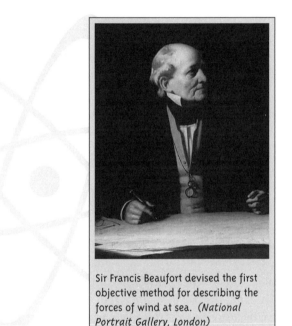

Sir Francis Beaufort devised the first objective method for describing the forces of wind at sea. *(National Portrait Gallery, London)*

Establishment of a Scale for Wind Force

Despite the many extraordinary advancements of modern technology, controlling the weather is a feat that may never be accomplished. The best people can do is try to plan around it. Useful planning requires knowledge of the current weather conditions, but simple descriptions such as "windy" may not provide enough information. A mild breeze provides perfect conditions for sailing or kite flying. More forceful winds might affect the decision of when to set out the trashcans for pickup. Winds strong enough to rip the siding off houses or overturn cars demand that people seek protective shelter. Precise descriptions of weather-related phenomena are particularly important for *maritime meteorology*, the study of the interactions of the sea and the atmosphere and the provision of weather services for sea-related activities. The safety of lives, the protection and efficient transport of valuable cargo, and the successful execution of military actions depend on weather conditions.

Sir Francis Beaufort was one of the greatest British *hydrographers.* He studied the physical conditions, boundaries, and flow of bodies of water for the British navy. He is notable for devising a method of describing wind forces that removed the ambiguity that had pestered sea-goers for centuries. The Beaufort wind force scale was first officially adopted by the British navy and then later adopted internationally.

False Records

Sir Francis Beaufort was the youngest son of Daniel Augustus and Mary Waller Beaufort. He was born on May 27, 1774, the fourth of seven children. Daniel was the rector of Navan, in County Meath, Ireland, but he was engaged in many different pursuits including geography, architecture, and landscaping. He was an accomplished topographer, admired for his skill at surveying by celestial observation. In 1792, he published the first complete, correct map of Ireland. Mary was intelligent and fluent in French and Italian as well as English. When Francis was two years old, the family moved from Navan to Mountrath, then to Wales, and later England.

The first grammar school Francis attended expelled him for having an undesirable accent. Around 1784 Francis was sent to Master David Bates's Military and Marine Academy in Dublin, where he learned mathematics and basic seamanship. Notebooks from his time at the academy show that he began recording astronomical observations when he was only 14 years old. In 1788, Francis's father sent him to Henry Ussher, a professor of astronomy at Trinity College in Dublin. Francis studied under Ussher for five months at the Dunsink Observatory, which had been founded only five years before. In 1789, the Beaufort family moved to London so Francis's father could publish his famous map of Ireland. Francis assisted his father by using his newly acquired skills to take latitude and longitude readings of the town of Athlone. By this time young Francis was already anxious to embark on a career at sea.

Daniel Beaufort made arrangements for an East India Company captain to hire Francis as his servant aboard the *Vansittart* on a trading and surveying voyage to the East Indies and China. On March 20, 1789, Francis Beaufort began his career at sea. He was horribly seasick at the beginning, but after that abated, he enjoyed ship life. Despite freshwater shortages, sailors with scurvy, and bad storms, Beaufort focused on marine life and practiced celestial navigation. He demonstrated his skill at this by correcting the charted latitude of Batavia, the Dutch East India Company operations headquarters. The previously charted latitude was off by three miles (4.8 km). After departing Batavia, the ship hit a sandbank while the crew was trying to take depth measurements. Damage to the ship forced the crew to land on a small island. They eventually had to abandon the ship, which held several chests of gold and silver as well as its cargo. The men were rescued by another ship from the same company and taken to China.

Having lost all his possessions and suffering a hernia, Beaufort reunited with his family in May 1790. The captain had been very pleased with Beaufort's service and recommended him for a position aboard a warship. He was appointed as "young gentleman" to Captain Albermarle Bertie aboard the frigate *Latona*. In order for Beaufort to obtain this position, records were fabricated to show that he had previously served as a midshipman (a person in training for a naval commission) on another boat from June 1787 to May 1788. He did not meet the requirements of being 18 years old and having three years of prior service at sea. Though falsifying the books was illegal, it was a common practice at the time.

A Passion for Sea Life

Beaufort was thrilled at the opportunity to serve on a warship. He had no privacy, hardly any free time, pitiable quarters, was bullied, and ate maggoty biscuits and old meat. Such was the life aboard a man-of-war, yet Beaufort did not complain. He looked forward to the possibility that the British might enter into a naval war with Spain. This never happened, though the event, known as the Spanish Armament, did serve to improve the condition of the Royal Navy.

In June 1791, Beaufort became a midshipman aboard the frigate, *Aquilon*, under Captain Robert Stopford. On the second day, Beaufort, who could not swim, fell overboard and had to be rescued. This was his second near-death experience at sea, and he was only 17 years old. After six months he was made a dickey, also called a master's mate. In this capacity he surveyed and made charts of the waters they sailed. He also took watch every eight hours, swept, wrote a daily journal for his master, and made sure the water, wine, and other provisions were distributed and stowed properly.

When Captain Stopford moved to the frigate *Phaeton*, Beaufort followed. As part of his naval training, Beaufort kept logbooks that were inspected as part of his exams. His books were meticulously kept and today are stored in the Meteorological Office Archives. He passed his exams to become a lieutenant in 1796.

Due to Stopford's successful exploits, Beaufort enjoyed steady income. His library grew as he purchased books on navigation and ships, astronomy, mathematics, the Bible, religious treatises, and Shakespeare. To compensate for his lack of formal education, he studied these books carefully.

When Stopford was promoted, Beaufort was made first lieutenant on the *Phaeton*. The new captain was James Nicoll Morris. In October 1800, while attacking a Spanish brig, the *San Josef*, Beaufort suffered 19 wounds, including three saber cuts and 16 slugs fired point blank at his left arm and side. Once again, he was near death but somehow he recovered. Three years passed before he regained effective use of his left arm. As a result of this incident, Beaufort was promoted to commander of the sloop *Ferret* in November, but the promotion was on paper only. He returned to England mid-year 1801 and was awarded a pension and half-pay. He was very disappointed. His dreams of commanding a fleet seemed forever out of his reach, but his body needed to heal.

The Need for Standard Weather Reporting

Beaufort was interested in all the sciences, including meteorology. Throughout his life he maintained a daily weather journal that included wind descriptions, temperatures, and barometric readings. Each of the king's thousand vessels was required to keep logbooks in which the wind and weather conditions were recorded every hour at the ship's current location. The books were deposited in the navy office. As a midshipman, Beaufort was required to record the weather every 12–24 hours, though he did so every two hours. He realized what a wealth of information all the navy's logbooks contained.

Weather was a significant factor in a seaman's life. The winds affected the oceanic currents, which affected a ship's direction and speed. Storms were dangerous and claimed many lives each year. Preparing for bad weather at sea was vital for safety reasons and predicting the weather was essential for such preparation. Examining the weather conditions that preceded historical bad storms was helpful for making predictions about possible future

Accurate weather reporting and prediction was particularly important at sea, as depicted by this ship struggling in a hurricane. *(Courtesy of the National Oceanic and Atmospheric Administration/Department of Commerce)*

storms. The importance of accurate weather reporting demanded a clear, unmistakable system for describing the conditions. Logbooks were filled, however, with subjective, ambiguous comments such as "fresh" or "moderate." A gale to one seaman might be considered a tempest to another.

Others who previously had attempted to classify the winds proposed scales that included 12–15 gradations, each having its own verbal description such as calm, gentle breeze, brisk gale, or storm. In 1759, the lighthouse engineer John Smeaton suggested a scale that defined wind speeds based on how fast it turned the sails of a windmill. Using an uncalibrated ordinary object such as a windmill as a meteorological instrument was a novel idea, one that Beaufort appreciated. Alexander Dalrymple, hydrographer to the British navy, thought Smeaton's scale was valuable. When he learned of Beaufort's desire to establish a more precise manner of weather reporting, he encouraged Beaufort to adapt a similar scale for use at sea.

What Moves the Air and the Water?

Wind is simply moving air. It is the basic attempt of the atmosphere to reach global pressure equilibrium. An air mass is a homogenous body of air, meaning its content has approximately the same temperature, pressure, and humidity. Air masses occupy large areas, often hundreds of square miles. Different regions of the Earth's surface absorb more sunlight than others. For example, during sunlight hours, land absorbs heat quicker than water, so the air above land is warmer. At night, the reverse is true—land cools quicker than water. This differential heating leads to differences in air pressure. Warmer air is less dense, and the molecules it contains move around more freely. As it rises, it creates air masses of lower pressure beneath the rising air. Cooler air descends, creating areas

A More Precise Scale

Beaufort was restored to active duty in June 1805 and given command of the *Woolwich*, an armed store ship. On this ship, Beaufort earned his lasting fame by devising a wind scale that bears his name. On January 13, 1806, while awaiting sailing orders at Portsmouth, Beaufort wrote in his private journal that from that date forward, he would use a more succinct and precise method for reporting the wind and weather conditions in his logbook. For all of the recorded weather information to be ultimately useful, it must be consistent. The same journal entry included his first draft of the Beaufort wind scale. The original scale included 14 descriptions of wind forces numbered zero through 13 and a list of alphabetical abbreviations for terms describing precipitation and cloud conditions. For example, *cl* denoted cloudy and *t*, thunder.

While using the numerical system and alphabetical abbreviations saved much space in the logbooks, the new method still did

of higher pressure. When two air masses with different pressures meet, the air molecules that are under higher pressure will move toward and into the mass of lower-pressure air in an attempt to equalize the difference. The greater the difference in air pressures between the two masses, the greater the force of the movement or of the wind created.

Understanding the formation and movement of wind is especially important for ship captains attempting to navigate the oceans, since wind affects the ocean currents, which can affect the direction and speed of a vessel. Currents are steady movements of water following a certain path. They are divided into two types, surface currents and deep currents. Surface currents are created by winds blowing across the water's surface, setting the water in motion. Landmasses help deflect the path of surface currents, causing them to be circular. Deep currents are controlled by variations in density of the water, which is affected by temperature and salinity, the level of salt dissolved in the water. Wind cycles also play a major role in driving deep oceanic currents.

Category	Description
0	Calm
1	Faint air, just not calm
2	Light airs
3	Light breeze
4	Gentle breeze
5	Moderate breeze
6	Fresh breeze
7	Gentle, steady breeze
8	Moderate gale
9	Brisk gale
10	Fresh gale
11	Hard gale
12	Hard gale with heavy gusts
13	Storm

ORIGINAL BEAUFORT WIND SCALE

Beaufort first proposed a wind force scale in his private journal on January 13, 1806.

not address the ambiguity. Remembering how Smeaton used a nonmeteorological object to describe gradations in wind force on land, the following year, Beaufort correlated his wind descriptions with the effect of the wind on the canvas sails of a fully rigged frigate of the period. The simplicity of the modified scale allowed even amateur observers to describe the wind forces objectively and consistently. Beaufort also added dots under the abbreviations to denote increased intensity of that condition. Over the years he continued improving his method of wind and weather reporting.

International Scale Adoption

During the next several years, Beaufort served on other ships, including the *Fredrikssteen*, on which he surveyed the coast of Karamania between 1811 and 1812. While in the eastern Mediterranean, he received an injury to the hip during a hostile encounter with the Turks. This injury forced Beaufort to retire from active sea duty, though he remained associated with the British navy for four more decades.

In 1829, Beaufort was appointed hydrographer to the navy. His responsibilities in this position were to survey waters, determine depths, and accurately chart the boundaries of different bodies of water. He finally began campaigning for his wind force scale to be officially adopted by the Admiralty by asking individual commanders of surveying ships to use his system. According to records, Captain Robert Fitzroy of the HMS *Beagle* was the first to employ

MODIFIED BEAUFORT WIND SCALE

Force	WMO classification	Appearance of wind effects		Wind velocity in knots
		On the sea	On the land	
0.	CALM	Sea appears mirrorlike	Calm; smoke rises vertically	Less than 1
1.	LIGHT AIR	Small ripples, no foam crests	Gentle smoke drift indicates wind direction	1–3
2.	LIGHT BREEZE	Small wavelets appear; crests do not break	Wind felt on face, leaves rustle, vanes move	4–6
3.	GENTLE BREEZE	Larger wavelets with occasional whitecaps	Leaves and small twigs moving; light flags extended	7–10
4.	MODERATE BREEZE	Smaller waves become longer, with frequent white caps	Dust, leaves, and paper lifted; small branches move	11–16
5.	FRESH BREEZE	Larger waves form, with whitecaps and spray	Small, leafy trees begin to sway	17–21
6.	STRONG BREEZE	Whitecaps are everywhere; there is more spray	Branches of large trees sway; whistling in wires	22–27
7.	NEAR GALE	Streaking white foam appears on the back of breaking waves	Whole trees move; resistance walking into the wind	28–33
8.	GALE	Larger waves become higher, with spindrift on breaking crests and extensive foam	Whole trees move; resistance walking into the wind	34–40
9.	STRONG GALE	Sea begins to roll with high waves and heavy foam	Light structural damage (shingles blow off roofs)	41–47
10.	STORM	Very high waves occur, and the sea appears white	Considerable structural damage, trees uprooted (rare occurrence on land)	48–55
11.	VIOLENT STORM	Exceptionally high waves occur; small and medium-size ships are not visible between crests		56–63
12.	HURRICANE	Sea is completely white with driving spray; visibility is poor, and the air is filled with spray		64–71
13.	HURRICANE			72–80
14.	HURRICANE			81–89
15.	HURRICANE			90–99
16.	HURRICANE			100–109
17.	HURRICANE			110–118

The original wind force scale was modified several times to include wind speeds and descriptions of the effect of wind on land as well as sea.

Beaufort's scale. Fitzroy used the scale in his logbooks on the historic voyage around South America with the young English naturalist Charles Darwin during the period 1831–36. Fitzroy later became the first director of what is now the Meteorological Office. By 1838, the Admiralty ordered all of its ships to use the Beaufort scale. Beaufort's scale lent such consistency to ship logbooks that the records were used as courtroom evidence in trials judging whether ship commanders acted appropriately in attack situations.

As time passed, the scale underwent more improvements. For example, when double topsails were introduced, adjustments had to be made. As *anemometers*, instruments used to measure wind speed, became more sophisticated, wind speeds were added to the scale. During the mid-1900s, the International Meteorological Committee further refined the scale by adding descriptions of the

Matthew Fontaine Maury

Matthew Fontaine Maury was an American meteorologist and oceanographer who was born on January 14, 1806, the same year that Beaufort developed his original wind scale. Maury's career in the U.S. Navy took him on oceanic expeditions all over the world. In 1842, he suffered from injuries incurred during a stagecoach accident and could no longer travel at sea. He was appointed superintendent of the Depot of Charts and Instruments and later became superintendent of the U.S. Naval Observatory. His duties included researching ocean winds, weather patterns, and ocean currents. Fortunately, the Beaufort wind scale was widely used by this time, so the newer logbooks were more consistent and therefore, meaningful to his research. To gather information, he urged naval and merchant marine captains from across the globe to send him their logbooks containing regular recordings of winds and other general weather conditions from their journeys. At first, very few complied with his request. Maury used the data he collected to chart ocean winds and currents, from which he recommended specific routes that optimized use

effects of wind on land and wind speeds as measured at a height of 10 feet (3 m) above the surface for each gradation.

Beaufort's Legacy

Under Beaufort's leadership, the *hydrography* office produced 1,500 new Admiralty charts. In 1846, Beaufort was made a rear admiral. He retired from the Admiralty in 1855, after serving for more than six decades. He died from old age two years later, in 1857. The development of a wind scale was not necessarily a highly intellectual endeavor, nor was it Beaufort's most significant lifetime accomplishment.

of the existing currents and winds. When word spread that by using Maury's charts, transoceanic voyage times were significantly reduced, many more captains started sending him their logbooks. In one example, travel time from England to Sydney, Australia, decreased from 250 to 130 days.

While working as a consultant in 1850, Maury charted ocean depths in order to recommend where to place the first transatlantic telegraph cable. While performing research for this project, he observed that the middle of the Atlantic was shallower than near the coasts. This helped lead to the discovery of the Mid-Atlantic Ridge. Maury was one of the organizers of the conference on meteorology and oceanography in Brussels in 1853. Discussion at this conference led to the eventual international adoption of the Beaufort wind scale. In 1855, Maury published the widely successful textbook, *The Physical Geography of the Sea*. Considered the first major textbook of oceanography, it contained the first systematic study of winds and oceanic currents, observations on surface temperatures of the Atlantic, bathymetric maps of the seafloor, and other valuable information. Maury left the U.S. Navy to join the Confederacy during the Civil War. After the war, he became a professor of meteorology at the Virginia Military Institute. He died on February 1, 1873.

The ingenuity of Beaufort's wind scale lay in its simplicity. Its cleverness impacted the field of maritime meteorology significantly, giving utility to large amounts of work already being done. The consistency it provided brought meaning to the meaningless.

Beaufort received many honors during his lifetime. In 1848, he was given the title of Knight Commander of the Bath for his civil service as hydrographer. He received an honorary doctorate degree from Oxford University. He was a fellow of the Royal Society of London, a fellow of the Astronomical Society, a member of the Royal Irish Academy, and a corresponding member of the Institute of France and of the U.S. Naval Lyceum. The sea north of Alaska was named in his honor.

In the 20th century, scales similar to the Beaufort scale were developed to describe hurricane and tornado intensities. The Saffir/Simpson hurricane scale is a five-point extension to the Beaufort scale that was introduced in 1969 by Herbert Saffir, a consulting engineer, and Robert Simpson, then the director of the National Hurricane Center. The Saffir/Simpson scale includes wind speed, coastal destruction potential, central pressure, and the height of the storm surge. The Fujita tornado intensity scale is a six-point scale used to classify tornadoes based on the degree of damage they cause and their wind speed. The Japanese-American meteorologist Tetsuya Theodore Fujita and his wife Sumiko introduced it in the 1970s. If mimicry is the highest form of praise, then Beaufort certainly earned his accolades.

CHRONOLOGY

1774	Sir Francis Beaufort is born on May 27 in Navan, County Meath, Ireland
1789	Joins the Dutch East India Company
1790	Enters the Royal Navy
1796	Is promoted to the rank of lieutenant
1800	Suffers 19 wounds in a successful attack on the Spanish ship, *San Josef* and earns a promotion to the rank of commander as well as a disability pension

1805	Receives first command, aboard the HMS *Woolwich*
1806	Outlines a scale for wind velocities in his private journal
1811–12	Beaufort travels to the Turkish coast on the HMS *Fredrikssteen* for a hydrography study and to patrol against pirates. During hostilities with the Turks, he is wounded in the hip and never returns to active sea duty
1817	Publishes his account of the Turkish expedition, *Karamania*
1829	Is appointed hydrographer to the Admiralty
1831–36	Captain Robert Fitzroy of the HMS *Beagle* is the first to use Beaufort's wind force scale in his ship's logbook
1838	Beaufort's wind scale is adopted officially by British Admiralty for all log entries
1846	Becomes rear admiral
1848	Is given the title of Knight Commander of the Bath in acknowledgment of his service as hydrographer
1855	Retires from the Admiralty
1857	Sir Francis Beaufort dies on December 17
1874	International Meteorological Committee adopts the Beaufort scale as a standard

FURTHER READING

Hamblyn, Richard. *The Invention of Clouds: How an Amateur Meteorologist Forged the Language of the Skies.* New York: Picador, 2001. Biography of Luke Howard, the man who developed a nomenclature system for clouds, but also contains a chapter on Beaufort's contribution to meteorology.

Heidorn, Keith C. "The Weather Legacy of Admiral Sir Francis Beaufort." Available online. URL: http://www.islandnet.com/~see/weather/history/beaufort.htm. Accessed February 8, 2005. Brief summary of Beaufort's career and contributions to meteorology.

Huler, Scott. *Defining the Wind: The Beaufort Scale, and How a Nineteenth-Century Admiral Turned Science into Poetry.* New York:

Crown Publishers, 2004. Depicts the history of the wind scale rather than its originator.

National Weather Service, Chicago. "The Beaufort Wind Scale." Available online. URL: http://www.crh.noaa.gov/lot/webpage/ beaufort. Accessed February 8, 2005. Description of the development and significance of the Beaufort Wind Scale.

Stephen, Leslie, and Sidney Lee, eds. *The Dictionary of National Biography.* Vol. 2. London: Oxford University Press, 1921–22. Brief account of lives and works of famous people from Great Britain in encyclopedia format.

Louis Agassiz

(1807–1873)

Louis Agassiz demonstrated the existence of a Great Ice Age. (*Courtesy of the National Oceanic and Atmospheric Administration*)

Proof for the Existence of a Great Ice Age

The distinction between weather and climate is often misunderstood. Weather refers to the conditions of the atmosphere with respect to indicators such as temperature, wind, and humidity, and it varies day-to-day, season-to-season, even within a specific location. Climate refers to the average weather conditions of an area over a period of time. The climate of 19th-century Europe was similar to the climate today. It was hard for people living in Switzerland back then to imagine that their continent had once been covered with a sheet of ice over one mile thick. Today it is known that the global climate cycles over periods of thousands of years. One man who was instrumental in illuminating to the world that the world's climate is not as it always has been was the Swiss-born naturalist Louis Agassiz. He earned his reputation as an ichthyologist (one who studies fish) but secured his place in scientific history by demonstrating that there was a Great *Ice Age*. He used geological evidence to convince the scientists of his day that a large portion of the Northern Hemisphere was once buried in ice.

Assistant to Cuvier

Jean Louis Rodolphe Agassiz was born on May 28, 1807, in Motieren-Vuly, Switzerland, to Rose Mayor Agassiz. His father, Rodolphe, in addition to the five previous generations of Agassiz men, was a Protestant minister. As a child, Louis enjoyed being outdoors, fishing with his bare hands, and exploring nature in his village by the Alps. He made cages and collected animals such as rabbits and snakes. As a man he would be passionate about his science, but as a child, his passion was sometimes misdirected. He once had the name of a cousin with whom he was enamored tattooed onto his arm in sulfuric acid. Another time he challenged his school's entire German club to duel against him for insulting the Swiss Club. He was an accomplished swordsman and beat four members before accepting their resignation with apology.

Louis performed well at school, particularly in languages and geography. He remained captivated by fish and even kept an aquarium fashioned from a granite boulder outside his home. He dissected them and even named a new species. At age 17, Louis started medical school in Zurich but was more interested in zoology than medicine. After two years at Zurich he enrolled at the University of Heidelberg, but then he transferred to Munich in 1827 with a friend named Alexander Braun. The lure of the distinguished faculty and the museum at Munich was appealing to an aspiring zoologist. A professor at the University of Munich asked Louis to assist in a project describing and classifying a collection of Brazilian fish.

This was quite an honor, but at the time it was rare to make a living as a naturalist, so though Louis accepted the task, he also continued with his medical studies. Though he was without a steady income, he hired an artist to engrave plates for the illustrations. From this project he published *Brazilian Fishes*, a volume dedicated to Georges Cuvier, a French anatomist considered the founder of vertebrate paleontology.

By the time Agassiz decided to go ahead and obtain his doctorate as well as his medical degree, the oral examination schedule at Munich was already filled. So he took his oral exams at the University of Erlangen and earned his doctorate in philosophy from the Universities of Munich and Erlangen in 1829. Interestingly, the topic of his doctoral dissertation was the superiority of woman to man. He argued that because woman was created last, she was more perfect. In 1830, he received his medical degree from Munich.

After obtaining his medical degree, Agassiz traveled to Paris in hopes of meeting two famous scientists, Cuvier and Alexander von Humboldt. Not only did he meet both men, but he also made favorable impressions. Cuvier was impressed by Agassiz's monograph on Brazilian fishes and offered him a space in his laboratory. Cuvier was a proponent of catastrophism, a theory asserting that sudden, violent, cataclysmic events shaped the history of the Earth. Such events were responsible for the formation of geological structures and the extinction of species. As a disciple of Cuvier, Agassiz subscribed to this same system of beliefs. Cuvier was impressed with Agassiz's efforts and offered him his entire collection of fishes and notes to classify and order in geological succession.

While in Paris, Agassiz also came to know Humboldt and was fascinated by his tales of South American adventure. Agassiz was short of money. Having to pay his artist was costly, and his family did not have the means to offer any financial support. One day Agassiz unexpectedly received a letter from Humboldt with a generous check enclosed. Shortly thereafter, Cuvier died, and Agassiz was left to worry about his future employment.

In 1832, Agassiz married Cécile Braun, the sister of his friend and former classmate, Alexander Braun. They eventually had two daughters and a son. His son, Alexander, also became a scientist. With a wife to support, a secure job was a necessity. On the recommendation of Humboldt, he was given a position as a professor of natural history at the Lyceum of Neuchâtel, about 12 miles (19.3 km) away from his hometown. Neuchâtel also opened a new museum that Agassiz directed. Agassiz was a fascinating, animated lecturer, but he also continued his work cataloging the fossil fish from Cuvier's immense collection. The resultant five-volume creation, *Récherches sur les poisons fossiles* (Research on fossil fish) was a valuable source of information. Appropriately, it was dedicated to Humboldt.

After the first volume came out, Agassiz received a letter from Charles Lyell, a Scottish geologist and then president of the Geological Society of London. The letter informed Agassiz that he was being awarded a Wollaston Medal for his work on fossil fishes. His work was not only useful to ichthyologists, but also to geologists. If a geologist found a fossil fish embedded in a layer of rock he was studying, he could refer to Agassiz's texts to learn whether that stratum was deposited in marine or freshwater and the geological time period during which it was deposited.

Studies on Glaciers

In 1834, Agassiz attended the Swiss Society of Natural Sciences annual meeting in Lucerne, Switzerland. At that meeting, a respected natural historian, Jean de Charpentier, presented a paper proposing that a *glacier* once covered Switzerland and even extended beyond. This was not a new idea. Other scientists had supposed that huge rocks scattered across northern Europe were brought there by glaciers. In 1829, a highway and bridge engineer named Ignace Venetz publicly proposed that glaciers had once covered Switzerland and other parts of Europe. Jean de Charpentier, who was director of the salt mines in Bex, was convinced by the evidence Venetz provided and took on the task of organizing and classifying the supporting evidence. Agassiz attended the meeting where Charpentier presented his paper on glacial theory but was not impressed.

Charpentier often invited scientists to his estate in Bex, located between the Alps and the Jura Mountains, near the entrance of the Rhône into the Lake of Geneva. Agassiz and his wife accepted an

Glaciers

A glacier is a huge dynamic body of ice. Glaciers may be a few hundred feet thick or up to two miles thick. If a glacier occurs over a mostly flat land surface, it is called a continental glacier, and it builds up in its middle, sloping outward in all directions. Glaciers such as those covering Antarctica and Greenland are called ice sheets. Smaller continental glaciers are called ice caps. As their name implies, valley glaciers fill mountain valleys. They are like long, slowly flowing rivers of ice. A chunk of ice that breaks off a glacier into the sea is called an *iceberg*. Icebergs can weigh up to 1 million tons.

Glaciers form when more snow falls than melts during a year. The accumulation is buried under the following year's accumulation and then crystallizes. The same happens the following year and so on. Finally, the weight of the many layers of snow crushes the crystallized snow into hard ice. This process is similar to what happens to the snow lining the side of a driveway during a long, snowy, cold winter. The snow is constantly shoveled off to the sides of the driveway. If the temperature never warms up enough to melt the snow, it continues getting piled up and packed down. After a while it no longer resembles snow but is harder and more compacted. Glacial ice is very dense and hard—hard enough to carve the sides of mountains like a pocketknife into a block of cheese. As long as more snow falls than melts each year, the glacier will grow, or advance. If temperatures increase and the glacial ice melts, the glacier is said to be retreating.

invitation during summer 1836. Charpentier showed him several great boulders that he believed were deposited by a glacier. The men hiked and climbed around the countryside and examined scratched rock surfaces and gravel deposits that Charpentier said

Glacial moraines. Both sides of Clear Creek in Colorado display lateral moraines three miles (4.8 km) long and averaging 500 feet (152 m) high. The granite walls of the canyon above are ground and polished, clear evidence of a past glacier. *(Courtesy of W. H. Jackson and the U.S. Geological Survey)*

were dropped by a melting glacier. On a tour of the Alps, Agassiz became convinced of the geological evidence supporting the previous existence of glaciers in Switzerland. The polished and smoothed cliffs could only be the result of a past glacier. He explored the Jura Mountains and found Alpine boulders and more polished and scratched surfaces. Charpentier was right; a huge glacier had extended all the way across the Swiss plains between the Alps and the Jura.

Charged with excitement, Agassiz traveled about trying to learn everything he could about glaciers and searching out additional evidence for their past existence. He found other large boulders, called erratics, in unusual locations. Some were larger than houses. They were composed of granite, yet the surrounding landscape was limestone. He observed other telltale signs such as mounds of grainy rocks at the ends and the sides of glaciers, called terminal and lateral *moraines*, respectively. Strikingly, he found similar accumulations where no glaciers were currently found. Another compelling observation was the presence of polished rocks with scratches or grooves in them.

Agassiz was convinced that in the past, glaciers had been much more extensive than they currently were. Glaciers could pick up boulders and transport them hundreds of miles over any terrain with ease. As glaciers melted, the boulders were deposited. As glaciers moved, they left behind trails of lateral moraines outlining their path. If they retreated, a terminal moraine was left behind. The weight of a flowing glacier ground and polished the rock below it like sandpaper. It scraped the walls of rocks of mountains as it passed, leaving grooves. Agassiz was certain an enormous glacier had once covered Switzerland, and it moved. Even more satisfying, the past existence of enormous glaciers was consistent with his catastrophic roots planted by Cuvier. He wondered if glaciers extended beyond Switzerland.

Resistance

Full of optimistic enthusiasm for his new idea of a universal glacier, Agassiz scrapped his planned presentation on fossil fishes for the Swiss Society of Natural Sciences annual meeting at Neuchâtel in 1837. He stayed up late the night before and prepared a new speech, which is referred to as his "Discourse of Neuchâtel." The audience was surprised to hear him introduce his paper by talking about erratic boulders and moraines rather than fish, but he continued with his speech. He described the evidence of glacial action across Switzerland. A sudden, catastrophic drop in temperature resulted in the ice, which destroyed all life in its way, creating a clean break between ancient and existing life-forms. When he stated that Alpine ice once extended from the Alps all the way up the southern slopes of the Jura, the audience became hostile. Then he proposed that a giant sheet of ice extended from the North Pole to the Mediterranean, and heated arguments broke out. Even Charpentier was shocked by such a sweeping claim.

The schedule for the remainder of the day was disrupted. Agassiz suffered frustrated amazement that his colleagues were so blind to what was now blatantly obvious to him. But Agassiz was the right person for the glacial spokesperson job. A situation that would have discouraged others made Agassiz even more determined. His fortitude and reputation gave him the power to speak out and be heard. Within 25 years, the reality of a Great Ice Age became universally accepted.

Part of the controversy at the time was religious in nature. Agassiz himself believed that God had caused the Great Ice Age as well as created all life, but others could not understand why God would create life only to freeze it to death. Some were just not ready to accept that the climate of their region was once so drastically different. Charles Lyell, a leading geologist of the time, offered an alternative for the placement of erratic boulders. He claimed they were frozen in icebergs and carried away from their original locations by floating great distances during the great flood. This idea was compatible with the biblical deluge and was the most widely accepted alternative theory. Compounding the problem of resistance was the overall ignorance of geologists about glaciers. At the time, the enormity of the Antarctic and the Greenland Ice Sheets had not yet been established. In addition, ice age theory was not compatible with the belief that the Earth was in the process of gradual cooling from its igneous formation. If the Earth were cooling, it would have been hotter, not colder as an ancient ice age would necessitate.

Agassiz persisted in his glacial studies. To examine glacial movement, he pummeled a series of stakes in a straight line into the glacial ice. Two years later, this line of stakes was shaped like the letter "U." The center stakes had traveled the fastest, since the movement of the stakes closest to the edges of the glacier was restricted due to friction. His team came across a cabin that had been built on top of a glacier on Mont Blanc in the Alps in 1827. The entire cabin had moved almost one mile (1.6 km) by 1839.

Glacial movement is not simply advancing and retreating. The pull of gravity on the heavy glacial ice causes the individual ice crystals to move, however sluggishly, like a river of cold molasses. Also, melting and refreezing of the ice helps the glacier move downslope. The upper layers of ice move more quickly than the lower layers. Furthermore, the middle, which encounters less friction than the edges, moves more quickly than the edges. Thus, the glacier actually flows like rivers do, just more slowly.

Undaunted by the continuing negative reactions to glacial theory, Agassiz published *Études sur les glaciers* (Studies on glaciers) in 1840. This was the first full-length review on glaciers. He summarized glacial motion, explaining how glaciers pushed moraines in front of them, carried boulders on top of them, and scratched and polished surfaces beneath them. Though this text was dedicated to Charpentier and Venetz, its printing ended the friendship between Charpentier and Agassiz. Charpentier was in the process of writing his own book, and he felt that Agassiz had betrayed him by jumping on his original ideas and publishing them first. A few years later, Agassiz was involved in another priority rift when Scottish physicist James Forbes accused him of stealing credit for the discovery of the phenomenon of alternating light and dark bands in glacial ice. These bands are called *ogives* and are an artifact of different flow rates between winter and summer.

In 1840, Agassiz presented a paper on glaciers at a meeting for the British Association for the Advancement of Science in Glasgow, Scotland. He claimed that northern Europe, northern Asia, and northern America were all once covered by ice. As it was three years before, the reaction was largely negative, including protests led by Lyell. One attendee, an English geologist named William Buckland, remained silent throughout the heated discussions.

After the meeting, Buckland met up with Agassiz and another geologist, Roderick Murchison. Together they surveyed Scotland and northern England for evidence of ancient glaciation and found it everywhere. Buckland was a crucial convert, as within months he was able to win over Lyell. In November 1840, Agassiz, Buckland, and Lyell all presented papers on evidence of glaciers across Britain at the Geological Society of London. Unbelievably, supporters of glacial theory still faced resistance, but in time truth would prevail.

Agassiz continued gathering evidence for glaciers to promote his cause. He was emotionally invested in the idea of a past glacial era. By 1845, most European geologists believed a huge glacier once covered Switzerland, but they still did not accept the idea of a universal ice age. In 1847, Agassiz published *Système glaciaire* (Ice systems). This text summarized all he had learned concerning glaciers:

How the Motions of the Earth Affect Its Climate

The axis of the Earth is an imaginary line through its center around which the planet rotates. Each rotation represents one 24-hour day. As the Earth rotates, it also orbits around the Sun following an elliptical pathway. This takes one calendar year. However, the axis of the Earth is not perpendicular to the elliptical orbit plane. The Earth is tilted about 23.5 degrees. Because of this, as the Earth rotates around the Sun, the Northern and Southern Hemispheres experience dissimilar seasonal climates. During *aphelion*, the Earth is farther from the Sun than at any other point in its orbit. Despite this, the Northern Hemisphere experiences its warmest season. This is because the planet is tilted so that the Northern Hemisphere faces the Sun most directly; therefore, the Sun's rays are very concentrated as they hit the Earth. In contrast, at *perihelion*, when the Earth is closest to the Sun, the Northern Hemisphere is pointed away from the Sun, so the rays that hit it are more diffuse and create less heat.

Such predictable seasonal weather changes are not sufficient to explain the changes in the Earth's climate that cultivated conditions capable of creating and sustaining an ice age. Milutin Milankovitch (1879–1958) was a Serbain geophysicist who developed a theory explaining how slight changes in geometry of the Earth's motions affect the amount of solar energy it receives, thus explaining the ice ages. The motions are cyclical and over long periods of time have a profound effect on the climate.

First, the pattern of the Earth as it orbits the Sun is generally described as slightly elliptical, with the Sun at the center. However, the orbital *eccentricity*, as it is called, actually varies from being elliptical to being nearly circular approximately every 100,000 years. Furthermore, as the

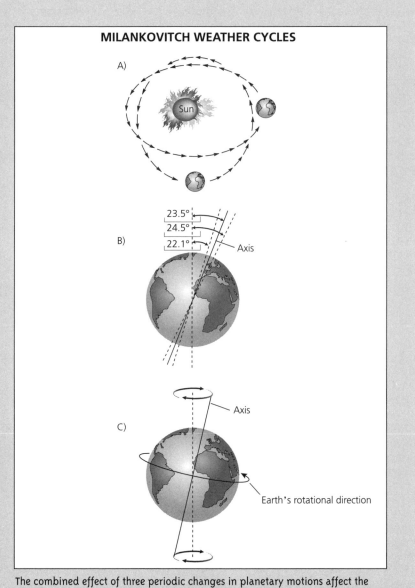

MILANKOVITCH WEATHER CYCLES

A)

B)

23.5°
24.5°
22.1°
Axis

C)

Axis

Earth's rotational direction

The combined effect of three periodic changes in planetary motions affect the global climate: (A) the pathway of the Earth's orbit, (B) the degree of its tilt, and (C) the wobble caused by the axial tilt.

(continues)

(continued)

pattern becomes less circular, the Sun becomes less centered. The changes in the shape of the orbit affect the distance between the Sun and the Earth during perihelion and aphelion by several million miles.

Second, the axial tilt, which is currently about 23.5 degrees, varies between 22.1 to 24.5 degrees every 40,000 years. As the tilt increases, the seasons become more intense, and extreme winters are difficult to escape. Snow and ice reflect the Sun's rays, which could bring warmth to melt the precipitation, back into space, keeping the Earth cold.

Lastly, the Earth behaves like a spinning toy top that becomes wobbly as it slows. It wobbles in a clockwise direction, tracing a full circle over a period of 21,000 years. This causes more extreme seasons in one hemisphere and less extreme seasons in the other.

The combined effect of these three cycles imparts significant modifications to global climate. In 1800, Milankovitch mathematically calculated the surface temperatures of the Earth during the past 600,000 years. He correlated these calculations with past ice ages and found a relationship between changes in the Earth's motion and position and major variations in the climate. While acceptance of Milankovitch's theory has varied over time, it remains the most plausible explanation for the Earth's glacial-*interglacial* shifts.

their appearance, their movement, the necessary climatic conditions, and the geographic conditions.

A One-Way Trip to the United States

With sponsorship from the king of Prussia, generated by Humboldt, Agassiz traveled to the United States on a mission to study its fauna for comparison with Europe's. He arrived at Boston in 1846 following an invitation to lecture at the Lowell Institute. His lecture series, "Plan of Creation in the Animal Kingdom," was well received. He even gave one lecture on glaciers in French. The following year he accepted a professorship at Lawrence Scientific School of Harvard University. Neuchâtel was disappointed to lose such a distinguished resident, but the United States was thrilled to claim the world's top naturalist as their own. The American people's regal treatment of Agassiz fed his ego. That, along with an entire new continent to study, convinced him to stay in the United States until his death.

Cécile never followed her husband to the United States. They suffered financial pressures, and she moved in with her brother Alexander in 1845, but Louis still loved her. He was deeply saddened by the news of her death in 1848. In 1850, he married Elizabeth Cabot Cary. She was an excellent companion and mother to his three children. She became a collaborator and writer for many of his American studies. After her husband's death, she became his biographer. She was a willful, intelligent woman, who is famous not only for her connection with Louis, but also for founding and becoming the first president of Radcliffe College, a women's educational institution. Radcliffe College officially merged with Harvard University in 1999 and is now called the Radcliffe Institute for Advanced Study at Harvard.

Agassiz traveled all over the United States, studying its natural environment. He planned a 10-volume study titled *Contributions to the Natural History of the United States*, but only four were published (1857–62). The most valuable information presented in this work was a comprehensive study of turtle embryology. These volumes were not especially successful, as by then many naturalists were embracing the ideas of Charles Darwin regarding evolution by natural selection. Agassiz was never able to accept these ideas, and in fact, he was an aggressive opponent of Darwin.

Agassiz remained a scientifically active researcher and popular teacher while in the United States. His contributions are too numerous and beyond the scope of this text to fully discuss them. Agassiz did determine that a lake once covered North Dakota, Minnesota, and Manitoba. Today it is called Lake Agassiz in his honor. He found sufficient evidence to extend his glacial theory to

North America. His large collection of data and fossils also led to the establishment of the Museum of Comparative Zoology (MCZ) at Harvard in 1859. This museum became a model for its design, which harmoniously blended teaching with research. Agassiz's influence drew extraordinary public and private financial support for this endeavor. In 1861, he was awarded the Copley Medal, the premier award of the Royal Society of London, for his eminent research in paleontology and other branches of science and particularly for *Poissons fossiles*. In 1865, he journeyed to Brazil, where he examined fauna and collected specimens for the Harvard museum.

Louis Agassiz died from a cerebral hemorrhage on December 14, 1873, in Cambridge, Massachusetts. Fittingly, a boulder from the Swiss glacier Aar was placed over his grave. His son Alexander became a well-respected marine biologist and also served as director of Harvard's MCZ. With his stepmother, he completed the unfinished fifth volume of *Contributions to the Natural History of the United States*. The establishment of the National Academy of Sciences (NAS) is also due to the efforts of this strong-willed man. Today the NAS remains a highly select organization, dedicated to the promotion and beneficial use of science and technology. It is their mandate to advise the federal government on scientific and technical matters. The MCZ and the NAS stand as an everlasting memory of Agassiz's dedication to the promotion of science, as do many geological monuments that bear his name. Though the idea of ancient enormous glaciers was not Agassiz's alone, his extension of the idea to a universal ice age and his willingness to take on the job of spokesperson earns him the distinction of "pioneer in science."

A Foundation for Paleoclimatology

Methods of *paleoclimatology*, the study of ancient climates, have improved since the mid-1800s. Today scientists can drill deep into the ice and cut out long cylinders called ice cores. The cores are multilayered, with each layer representing a unit of time. The deeper the layer, the older the ice. Analysis of the individual layers reveals evidence about the climate at the time the layer was formed. For example, the ratio of different isotopes of oxygen allows scientists to estimate the temperature when the layer was formed.

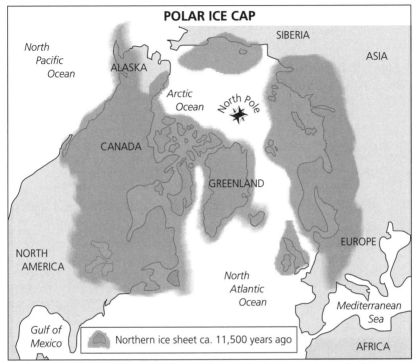

POLAR ICE CAP

SIBERIA

North
Pacific
Ocean
ALASKA

ASIA

Arctic
Ocean

North Pole

CANADA

GREENLAND

EUROPE

NORTH
AMERICA

North
Atlantic
Ocean

Mediterranean
Sea

Gulf of
Mexico

Northern ice sheet ca. 11,500 years ago

AFRICA

During the most recent ice age, the northern polar ice cap extended all the way into the British Isles and North America.

Bubbles trapped in the frozen ice contain samples of the atmospheric gas composition, which is indicative of relative temperatures. Also, higher levels of dust present in a sample indicate the climate was cold and windy. Sediment samples from the ocean floor also provide much evidence about the climate at the time the sediment layer was deposited.

Using these and other modern methodologies, paleoclimatologists have determined that there have been about two dozen ice ages during the past two and one-half million years. Average global temperatures dropped, and the polar ice caps expanded. The most recent ice age, named the Great Ice Age, began approximately one-half million years ago and lasted until 11,500 years ago. The Earth is currently experiencing an interglacial period, a period between glacial periods. Though the idea of past ice ages is commonplace today, in the mid-1800s there was much resistance to accepting this. Louis Agassiz himself ignored the idea the first time it was presented to him. After gathering evidence, he could no longer deny the facts and was instrumental in convincing others to open their own eyes. By providing the scientific proof for the existence of a Great Ice Age, Agassiz changed scientists' understanding of the Earth's climate and paved the way for paleoclimatologists to investigate the globe's cyclical nature of warming and cooling.

CHRONOLOGY

1807	Louis Agassiz is born on May 28 in Motieren-Vuly, Switzerland
1829	Earns doctorate of philosophy from the University of Munich and the University of Erlangen
1830	Earns medical degree from University of Munich
1831-32	Works with French anatomist Georges Cuvier in Paris
1832	Becomes professor of natural history at College of Neuchâtel in Switzerland
1833-44	Publishes five-volume series on fossil fishes, *Récherches sur les poisons fossiles* (Research on fossil fish)
1835-45	Studies glacial formations of Switzerland
1837	Gives inaugural address as president of the Swiss Society of Natural Sciences, "Discourse of Neuchâtel," introducing radical ice age theory
1840	Publishes *Études sur les glaciers* (Studies on glaciers)
1846	Travels to America to lecture at the Lowell Institute in Boston
1847	Accepts professorship at Lawrence Scientific School, Harvard University, and publishes *Système glaciaire* (Ice systems)
1857-62	Publishes the four-volume *Contributions to the Natural History of the United States*
1859	Establishes the Harvard Museum of Comparative Zoology

| 1863 | Convinces colleagues to establish the National Academy of Sciences |
| 1873 | Dies on December 14 in Cambridge, Massachusetts |

FURTHER READING

Agassiz, Elizabeth Cary. *Louis Agassiz, His Life and Correspondence.* Boston, Mass.: Houghton Mifflin, 1893. A memoir written by his talented and beloved wife.

Bolles, Edmund Blair. *The Ice Finders: How a Poet, a Professor, and a Politician Discovered the Ice Age.* Washington, D.C.: Counterpoint, 1999. A saga describing the contributions of Elisha Kent Kane, Louis Agassiz, and Charles Lyell in discovering the existence of a Great Ice Age, written in plain language.

Lurie, Edward. *Louis Agassiz: A Life in Science.* Baltimore and London: Johns Hopkins University Press, 1988. Thorough account of Agassiz's contributions in geology, paleontology, and zoology and detailed account of his life and work in the United States.

Olson, Richard, ed. *Biographical Encyclopedia of Scientists.* Vol. 1. New York: Marshall Cavendish, 1998. Clear, concise summary of major events in the scientists' lives at an accessible level.

University of California, Berkeley Museum of Paleontology. "Louis Agassiz (1807–1873)," Available online. URL: http://www.ucmp.berkeley.edu/history/agassiz.html. Accessed February 8, 2005. Brief biographical sketch and outline of Agassiz's scientific thoughts.

William Ferrel

(1817–1891)

William Ferrel explained the complex
mechanics of the general circulation
of the atmosphere. *(Courtesy of
NOAA Central Library)*

Effect of the Earth's Rotation on
Atmospheric and Oceanic Circulation

William Ferrel was an intellectual genius who began his career as
a country school teacher. His greatest works focused on the
Earth's rotation, tidal matters, and related meteorological subjects. He was the first to apply mathematical formulas concerning
moving bodies to the meteorological phenomena of atmospheric
and oceanic circulation. The most significant contribution of his

research to meteorology was the formulation of a law that described the deflection of a body moving along the surface of the Earth due to the Earth's rotation. In the northern atmosphere, the deflection occurs to the right, and in the southern atmosphere, the deflection occurs to the left. Today this is known as Ferrel's law.

Mathematics on a Barn Door

William Ferrel was born to Benjamin Ferrel and his wife, whose maiden name was Miller, on January 29, 1817, in Bedford (now Fulton) county, Pennsylvania. As a boy, William attended the local school and helped his large family by working at his father's sawmill. In 1829, the family moved to a farm in what is now West Virginia. William attended a one-room schoolhouse for two winters and proved to be very bright. Due to the lack of other available sources, he read the scientific entries in the local weekly newspaper. When he was 15 years old, he came across and devoured a book on advanced arithmetic, a defining event of his formative years.

During that same year, William witnessed a partial solar eclipse, an event where the Moon passes in between the Earth and the Sun. This astronomical event left such an impression on young William, that one and one-half years later, he mathematically predicted the eclipses for the year 1835 using information he gleaned from old copies of farmers' almanacs and an elementary geography book. This was quite remarkable for a primarily self-educated teenager.

At age 17, while working full-time on his father's farm, William obtained a copy of a surveying text that included some trigonometry. He mastered the contents over the course of a summer, drawing geometric diagrams with a pitchfork on the wooden barn doors as a study aid. His desire to learn more increased. Geometry was the next logical subject to master, and he did just that the following year after borrowing a geometry text from a surveyor who lived nearby. When he was 20 years old, he learned about the law of gravitation and that the Moon and planets moved in elliptical orbits.

Using money he earned by teaching, Ferrel entered Marshall College in Mercersburg, Pennsylvania, in 1839. At Marshall, he was exposed to algebra for the first time and received his first formal training in mathematics. Prior to this experience, he simply taught himself whatever was necessary to answer the questions his mind put forward. Unfortunately, the money he had saved up to defray expenses ran out prematurely, and he had to interrupt his education after only two years at Marshall. After teaching for a while to earn more money, Ferrel entered Bethany College in West Virginia in 1842. He graduated two years later and moved to Liberty, in western Missouri, to teach there.

The Newton of Meteorology

In Liberty, Ferrel came upon a copy of Isaac Newton's *Principia*, which more fully described the law of universal gravitation and the elliptical orbits of the planets. The law of universal gravitation states that every object in the universe attracts every other object with a force that is proportional to the product of their masses and inversely proportional to the square of the distance between them. Newton also mathematically explained the existence of ocean tides. The edition included several supplementary papers about tides. Finding this text in the small town of Liberty was a godsend for Ferrel. Reading *Principia* kept him thinking about science; in particular, it started him thinking about tides.

In 1850, after accepting a position teaching in Todd County, Kentucky, Ferrel learned that the French astronomer and mathematician Simon Laplace had written extensively about tides in the five-volume work, *Méchanique céleste* (Celestial mechanics). Laplace observed that the Moon was accelerating faster than existing calculations predicted. He suggested the faster acceleration was due to changes in the Earth's orbit from gravitational pulls of other planets. After studying Newton, Ferrel came to the conclusion that the action of the Moon and Sun on the tides must retard the Earth's rotation on its axis. Laplace did not account for retardation of the Earth's rotation by the tides, however, and his calculations seemed to work out. Ferrel supposed the effect he anticipated was accounted for by the Earth's gradual contraction due to cooling. Ferrel's first scientific work, "The Effect of the Sun and Moon upon the Rotary Motion of the Earth," was published in *Gould's Astronomical Journal* in 1853. The paper mathematically demonstrated how the tides affected the rotation of the Earth and the Moon.

Tides

Tides are the alternate rising and falling of the surface of the ocean. They result from the gravitational attraction of the Moon and the Sun. The Moon's gravity pulls at the ocean waters on the side of the Earth facing it. This causes a slight bulge, or distortion outward, and the water in that area is deeper. At the same time, the Moon's gravity also acts to pull the solid Earth away from the water on the far side of the Earth, that is, the side facing away from the Moon. These lunar bulges account for high tide. Simultaneously, low tide results in portions of the Earth located at 90-degree angles to the high tide bulges. The Sun exerts a similar effect, but since it is much farther away from the Earth than the Moon, its effect is approximately one-half that of the Moon. In most places, tidal cycles are semidiurnal, meaning there are two tidal cycles each day.

Because the Earth rotates on its axis at the same time as the Moon revolves around the Earth, it takes slightly longer than 24 hours for the Moon to return to the same relative position above the Earth each day. As a result, high and low tides occur at different times every day. Tides rise and fall up to 10 feet (3 m), sometimes more. Tidal currents are caused by the tidal action of the ocean water. These currents are relatively weak but are stronger near land.

Ferrel established his own private school in Nashville, Tennessee, in 1854. Nashville was the first city in which Ferrel had lived. He no longer had to depend upon the occasional journeys of friends and neighbors to nearby cities to obtain books or other scientific treatises. With easier access to other volumes about tides and the Earth, Ferrel came to the conclusion that Laplace's work on the Moon's acceleration was flawed. Laplace had failed to account for what mathematicians refer to as second-order terms in his calculations concerning the effect of tides on the Earth's rate of rotation about its axis. In 1856, Ferrel published a paper, "The Problem of the Tides with Regard to Oscillations of the Second Kind," addressing this issue in *Gould's Astronomical Journal.* He also claimed that Laplace was incorrect in stating that diurnal tides (tides with a single high-tide stage and a single low-tide stage each day) would disappear in an ocean of uniform depth. In 1864, Ferrel returned to the problem of tidal friction, which had been ignored by Laplace, in a lecture to the American Academy of Arts and Sciences. This was the first quantitative treatment on the subject of fluid friction. By challenging the world-renowned Laplace, Ferrel proved himself an intellectual force.

The Effect of Rotation on Moving Bodies

The focus of Ferrel's studies naturally shifted from tidal action to meteorology. Ferrel's most significant contribution to science was his explanation of the effect of the Earth's rotation on the movement of bodies at its surface. He showed how wind circulation patterns and ocean currents were affected by the Earth's rotation. By reading Matthew Fontaine Maury's *The Physical Geography of the Sea*, Ferrel learned that belts of high pressure exist at 30 degrees latitude. Belts of low pressure exist at the *equator* and the *poles*. This distribution interested Ferrel. He related what he learned about the connection between the Earth's rotation and the movement of the tides with the motion of the atmosphere. These studies led to his paper that described wind circulation patterns in middle latitudes, "Essay on the Winds and Currents of the Ocean," published in the *Nashville Journal of Medicine* in 1856. Ferrel rejected previous unsubstantiated hypotheses about winds, pressures, and storms. He showed that such meteorological phenomena were explainable by a few simple natural laws. Ferrel demonstrated how atmospheric motions and ocean currents were deflected by the Earth's rotation. He used this premise to develop a model for general atmospheric circulation and the rotary action of cyclones. He also proposed the existence of a wind circulation *cell* at middle latitudes.

The *three-cell model* is a simplified explanation of atmospheric circulation that summarizes the effects of the Earth's surface winds. The model consists of three different types of circulation cells. Convection-driven *Hadley cells* occur near the equator where warmer air rises and loses moisture in the process. The air moves away from the equator and then warm, dry air descends in the tropics. *Polar cells* occur over higher latitudes. Air circulates away from the poles near the surface of the Earth and then rises as it reaches middle latitudes and travels back toward the poles. Unlike Hadley and polar cells, which are driven by surface temperatures, *Ferrel cells* are indirectly driven by the Hadley and polar cells. They exist at middle latitudes in between the Hadley and polar cells. Within a Ferrel cell, air rises at the *polar front* and then descends in the tropics. Ferrel's theory was not precisely correct, but it was the first reasonable attempt to explain the westerly winds in the middle latitudes.

In 1857, the *American Ephemeris and Nautical Almanac* hired Ferrel to perform a number of intricate computations. Ferrel brought the work back to Nashville, but in 1858, he left the school that he established and moved to Cambridge to work for the almanac full-time. After teaching grammar school for 15 years, he

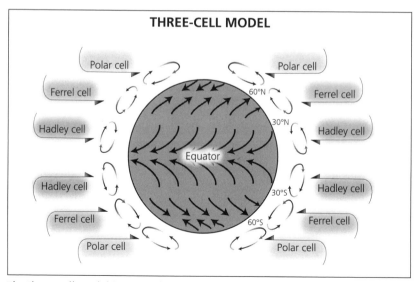

The three-cell model is a popular representation for explaining atmospheric circulation.

was finally able to devote all his efforts to scientific research. At the request of friends, he published an extension of his 1856 essay in *Mathematical Monthly*. The expanded paper, titled "The Motions of Fluids and Solids Relative to the Earth's Surface," was Ferrel's most significant contribution to the science of meteorology. This work earned him the title of founder of geophysical fluid dynamics (a title he shared with Laplace) and firmly established what is referred to today as Ferrel's law. Ferrel's law states that if a body is moving in any direction, there is a force, arising from the Earth's rotation, which always deflects it to the right in the Northern Hemisphere, and to the left in the Southern Hemisphere. This theory was published for a wider audience in the *American Journal of Science* in 1861. Ferrel deduced the relationship between the winds and the pressure gradients and explained the resistance of the Earth's surface to the winds. He also described the role of currents in the upper atmosphere in the development and motions of storms.

In 1857, the Dutch meteorologist Christoph H. D. Buys Ballot also described wind circulation in areas of high and low pressures. Buys Ballot said if you stand with your back toward the wind in the Northern Hemisphere, there is an area of low pressure on your left. If you are in the Southern Hemisphere, the area of low pressure will be on your right. When Buys Ballot learned of Ferrel's prior work, he acknowledged Ferrel's claim for the discovery.

Tide-Predicting Machine

In 1867, Ferrel moved to Washington to accept a position with the U.S. Coast and Geodetic Survey. Once again, his research focused on tides. He published *Tidal Researches* as an appendix to the Coast Survey Report in 1874. He next worked on a series of papers, titled "Meteorological Researches for the Use of the Coast Pilot," that were published as appendices to the *Report of the Superintendent of the U.S. Coast Survey for 1875*.

In the 1870s, Ferrel refined the interpretations of the American meteorologist James P. Espy, who theorized about the creation of atmospheric disturbances such as storms. Espy's convection theory stated that storm formation begins with warm air rising and expanding, which causes cooling. The decrease in temperature causes vapor

Coriolis Effect

The rotation of the Earth about its axis does not cause wind. The Earth's atmosphere is held in place and rotates in conjunction with the Earth. However, the eastward rotation of the Earth does affect the paths of the wind. This is referred to as the Coriolis effect, named after the French physicist and mathematician who mathematically explained it. In 1835, Gaspard-Gustave de Coriolis had published a paper, "Sur les équations du mouvement relatif des systèmes de corps" (On the equations of relative motion of systems of bodies). This paper described motion on a spinning surface, such as the rotating Earth. Though the phenomenon is called the Coriolis effect, Ferrel was the first to work out the meteorological implications in 1856.

The Coriolis effect describes how, in the Northern Hemisphere, air masses appear deflected to the right of the original path, and in the Southern Hemisphere, to the left. The apparent deviation is due to the rotation of the Earth. The wind itself has not changed path, it simply appears that way since the Earth moved. The effect is greatest at the North and South Poles, and no effect is observed at the equator. This is because the rotation of the Earth diminishes as the poles are approached. To illustrate this point, consider that in a single day, one complete rotation of the Earth causes a point on the equator to travel almost 25,000 miles (40,000 km), the circumference of the Earth. However, a point further north or south does not travel as far in the same amount of time, thus the velocity at that point is slower. As air moves north from the equator, it retains its faster velocity, causing it to

in the air to condense, forming clouds. This process of convection causes areas of low pressure to develop underneath. High pressure air flows inward and upward, leading to heavy rainfall. Espy erroneous-

move eastward in comparison to the slower-moving surface underneath it. The forces that seem to push the air and water eastward when moving away from the equator are called Coriolis forces, and they are responsible for the spinning motion of hurricanes and tornadoes. The Coriolis effect is most apparent with winds moving longitudinally, that is, in the north-south direction. Coriolis forces differ according to speed. Faster winds exhibit a greater deflection since greater distances are covered during a given time period.

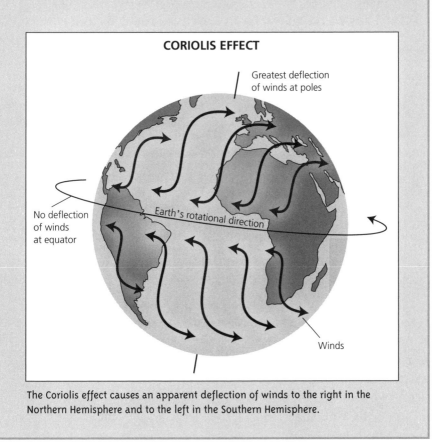

CORIOLIS EFFECT

Greatest deflection of winds at poles

No deflection of winds at equator

Earth's rotational direction

Winds

The Coriolis effect causes an apparent deflection of winds to the right in the Northern Hemisphere and to the left in the Southern Hemisphere.

ly proposed that winds blew in from all directions toward a storm center but correctly suggested that the condensation of ascending vapor was the source of energy for such storms. Ferrel examined the roles of moisture and general air circulation in the formation of storms. He elaborated on Espy's studies on cyclones and applied his knowledge concerning the effects of friction. He also extended Espy's ideas to thunderstorms and tornadoes as well as hurricanes. Ferrel explained that the centrifugal force of a whirling storm accounted for the low pressure within its center.

While working for the U.S. Coast Survey, Ferrel also presented a model for a tide-predicting machine. The mechanical device simulated the motions that caused the tides and gave maxima and minima of tidal heights rather than a continuous curve as did the machines already in use. He read a paper describing the machine at the annual American Association for the Advancement of Science meeting in Boston in 1880. The machine was constructed and put into service in 1883. Over the next 25 years, it was used to predict tides for the Coast Survey's "Tide Tables." Today computers are used to predict times and heights of tides.

From 1882 until 1886, Ferrel worked as a professor of meteorology for the U.S. Army's Signal Service (which became the U.S. Weather Bureau in 1891). In his later years, he published several works on meteorology for more general audiences. These included *Popular Essays on the Movements of the Atmosphere* (1882), *Temperature of the Atmosphere and the Earth's Surface* (1884), *Recent Advances in Meteorology* (1886), and *A Popular Treatise on the Winds* (1889). At age 70, Ferrel retired to spend the last years of his life with his brothers and sisters.

The chief founder of geophysical fluid dynamics died in 1891, at age 74, in Maywood, Kansas. Ferrel had been a reserved man but was highly esteemed by his peers. In his autobiography, Ferrel admitted to being too shy to read a paper on tidal friction though he knew it contained important and original information. He carried it with him to several meetings of the American Academy at Boston before he summoned the courage to present it publicly. During his lifetime, Ferrel was awarded honorary master's and doctorate degrees. In 1868, he was elected to the prestigious National Academy of Sciences. He also was an associate fellow of the American Academy of Arts and Sciences and an honorary member of meteorological societies in Austria, Britain, and Germany.

In a biographical memoir of Ferrel, Cleveland Abbe stated that Ferrel gave "the science of meteorology a foundation in mechanics as solid as that which Newton laid for astronomy." Ferrel's application of mathematics to meteorology was pioneering and helped meteorologists embrace mathematics as an integral part of their research. For his comprehensive description of general atmospheric circulation, he remains one of America's most eminent and original meteorologists.

CHRONOLOGY

1817	William Ferrel is born on January 29 in Bedford (now Fulton) County, Pennsylvania
1832	Witnesses a partial solar eclipse of the Sun, inspiring him to learn more about astronomy
1839	Enters Marshall College in Mercersburg, Pennsylvania. After two years, he runs out of money and returns to teaching
1842–44	Completes his education at Bethany College in West Virginia
1844–50	Teaches school in Liberty, Missouri
1850	Ferrel reads Newton's *Principia* for the first time. The edition contained additional resources on the subject of tides
1850–54	Teaches school in Todd County, Kentucky
1853	Ferrel writes his first scientific paper, "The Effect of the Sun and Moon upon the Rotary Motion of the Earth," describing how the action of the Moon and the Sun on the tides affects the Earth's rotation on its axis, contradicting popular theory proposed originally by Laplace
1854	Starts own school in Nashville, Tennessee
1856	Publishes "Essay on the Winds and Currents of the Ocean" in the *Nashville Journal,* stating that the motion of air and water along lines of constant pressure were due to the Earth's rotation

1858–67	Works for the *American Ephemeris and Nautical Almanac,* an annual U.S. Navy Nautical Office publication
1859–60	Ferrel publishes his most significant contribution to meteorology, "The Motions of Fluids and Solids Relative to the Earth's Surface," in *Mathematical Monthly,* earning him the title of founder of geophysical fluid dynamics and firmly establishing what is referred to today as Ferrel's law
1864	Gives the first quantitative treatment of tidal friction
1867	Moves to Washington to work for the U.S. Coast and Geodetic Survey
1874	Publishes *Tidal Researches* as an appendix to the Coast Survey Report for that year
1878–81	Publishes three treatises, "Meteorological Researches for the Use of the Coast Pilot"
1880	Presents model for a tide-predicting machine
1882–86	Accepts a position with the U.S. Army Signal Service and continues supervising the production of the tide-predicting machine
1882–89	Publishes several works on meteorology for a general audience
1883	Tide-predicting machine is put into service and is used to predict the tides by the U.S. Coast and Geodetic Survey for the next 25 years
1891	Dies on September 18 in Maywood, Kansas

FURTHER READING

Biographical Memoirs. National Academy of Sciences. Vol. 3. Washington, D.C.: National Academy of Sciences, 1895. Fullest memoir of Ferrel, written by a distinguished colleague for the premier scientific organization of the United States. This volume also contains Ferrel's autobiography, written at the request of a friend.

Cox, John D. *Storm Watchers: The Turbulent History of Weather Prediction from Franklin's Kite to El Niño.* Hoboken, N.J.: John Wiley, 2002. Highlights the work of early weathermen and outlines the evolution of weather forecasting.

Garraty, John A., and Mark C. Carnes, eds. *American National Biography.* Vol. 7. New York: Oxford University Press, 1999. Brief account of lives and works of famous Americans in encyclopedia format.

National Oceanic and Atmospheric Administration (NOAA). "William Ferrel (1817–1891)," Available online. URL: http://www.moc.noaa.gov/fe/ferrel.htm. Updated May 3, 2000. Brief biography of the man for whom the NOAA ship *Ferrel* was named.

John Tyndall

(1820–1893)

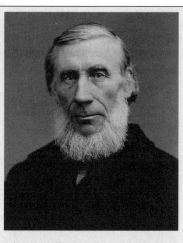

John Tyndall researched the effects of atmospheric gases on radiant heat. *(Library of Congress, Prints and Photographs Division [LC-USZ62-94025])*

The Effect of Invisible Gases on the Earth's Temperature

On a clear night, the beam of light radiating from a car's headlights is not visible from the side of the road; one must be in front of the source to view it. If the weather is foggy, however, the beam is visible because the light is scattered by the excess water vapor molecules suspended in the air. This phenomenon is the *Tyndall effect*, named after John Tyndall, a 19th-century scientist who researched atmospheric gases and the transmission of radiation. He found that the most abundant components of the atmosphere had the least effect on the transmission of radiant heat through it, while trace amounts of invisible gases had an enormous effect on the Earth's surface temperature. Water vapor, in particular, efficiently absorbed heat radiation. Tyndall suggested that changes in climate could be traced back to variations in levels of water vapor and carbon dioxide. As a natural philosopher, Tyndall did not limit himself to a single scientific focus; throughout his life he studied numerous subjects ranging from electromagnetism to bacteriology.

Surveyor, Lecturer, Fellow

John Tyndall was born to Sarah Macassey Tyndall at Leighlinbridge, County Carlow, Ireland, on August 2, 1820. John Tyndall, Sr., was a member of the Irish Constabulary and did his best to support John's early education by mending boots to supplement his meager income. Through attending the local national school and then private tutoring, John developed a strong enough background in mathematics to join the Ordnance Survey of Ireland as a surveyor and draftsman in 1839. Because of his fine skills, after three years he was chosen to join the English Ordnance Survey, and in 1844, he began working as a railway surveyor. Whenever possible, he attended the mechanics' institute lectures at Preston in Lancashire.

Tyndall began teaching mathematics in 1847 at Queenwood College. The following year he traveled to Germany to study chemistry and physics at the University of Marburg. His drive toward learning and his mathematical dissertation on the geometry of screw surfaces led to a doctorate in only two years. After spending a little time in Berlin, he returned to Queenwood College as a lecturer in mathematics and natural philosophy until 1853, when he began his association with the Royal Institution of Great Britain, an institution founded in 1799 that is dedicated to science research and communication. He became close friends with Michael Faraday, superintendent of the Royal Institution, and under Faraday's direction he became an outstanding lecturer and research scientist. When Faraday died in 1867, Tyndall assumed his position and wrote an extensive scientific memorial, *Faraday, as a Discoverer* (1868), to honor his role model.

Tyndall began his research career investigating the subjects of magnetism and diamagnetic polarity, which he studied from 1850–55. Magnetism is the branch of physics related to magnets and magnetic properties, including the exertion of attractive or repulsive forces on other materials. Diamagnetism is a weak form of magnetism in which materials take a position at right angles to the lines of force of an external magnetic field. Tyndall's work on the magnetic properties of crystals, their crystalline molecular structure, and the effect of compression on them came to the attention of the scientific community, and in 1852, he was elected a fellow of the prestigious learned organization, the Royal Society of London. In 1853, Tyndall gave an invited lecture titled "On the Influence of Material Aggregation upon the Manifestations of Force" at the Royal Institution. The members were so impressed with Tyndall's ability to engage the audience and explain scientific concepts that they invited him back, and within three months they appointed him professor of natural philosophy.

Glacial Motion

On the way back from attending a British Association meeting in 1854, Tyndall visited the slate quarries of Penrhyn, where he observed the cleavage patterns. He used his knowledge about the effects of mechanical pressure on crystals to surmise that pressure caused the cleavage of the slate rocks. These studies led to a trip to the Alps to study the structure of the glacier ice. From 1857 to 1860, Tyndall explored the motion of glaciers, massive rivers of shifting ice. Unlike snow, the crystals of ice in glaciers are all bound together, giving it rigidity and causing scientists to wonder how glaciers moved. Did they flow like a liquid or slide more like a solid? Was the shifting due to slow melting and refreezing of the glacial ice or expansion and contraction? After several trips to the Alps to make observations, take measurements, and analyze the structure and properties of the ice under pressure, Tyndall suggested the apparent movement was due to fracture (forming crevasses) and *regelation* (a process in which ice

Father of the Greenhouse Theory

The chemist Svante August Arrhenius was born in February 19, 1859, in Vik, near Uppsala, Sweden. He received the Nobel Prize in chemistry in 1903 for his development of the electrolytic theory of dissociation (ionization) that he first presented as his doctoral thesis at Uppsala University in 1884. He proposed that when electrolytes were dissolved in water, they dissociated into separate positively and negatively charged ions that carried an electric current during electrolysis. He later described the influence of electrolytic dissociation on the osmotic pressure, melting points, and boiling points of solutions containing them and the biological consequences of dissociated ions.

Arrhenius was interested in other topics of physics as well, including cosmic physics, the physics of the Earth, sea, and the atmosphere. He recognized the significant role of trace constituents in the atmosphere as demonstrated by Tyndall's research. In 1895, Arrhenius presented a paper

melts under pressure then subsequently refreezes), a controversial view that conflicted with the popular theory that glacier ice was viscous, championed by James D. Forbes from Edinburgh. Tyndall published his observations in *Glaciers of the Alps* in 1860, and though his observations were not conclusive, his studies helped advance the currently prevailing theories. Tyndall enjoyed exploring the mountains and became an accomplished mountaineer, earning the distinction of being the first person to climb the Weisshorn in 1861.

Radiant Heat

The main research for which meteorologists remember Tyndall is his work on atmospheric gases that began in 1859 and continued on and off for 12 years. To measure the absorptive properties of differ-

to the Stockholm Physical Society that claimed changes in the content of carbon dioxide (CO_2) were responsible for glacial advances and retreats. Published in *Philosophical Magazine* the following year, "On the Influence of Carbonic Acid in the Air upon the Temperature of the Ground" purported that very small changes in trace atmospheric components affected the total amount of heat energy present near the Earth's surface. The model he described accounted for the onset of interglacials and ice ages as determined by geologists. Noticing that the amount of carbon dioxide in the atmosphere was increasing due to the burning of fossil fuels, he explained a carbon dioxide theory of climate and introduced the hothouse theory of the atmosphere. He calculated that without the *greenhouse effect*, the Earth's average temperature would be about –100°F (–73°C), cold enough to freeze the oceans. Because of his research, he has been called the father of the greenhouse theory.

Arrhenius became a professor of physics at Stockholm's Högskola (later the University of Stockholm) in 1895 and also served as rector from 1897 until 1905, when he became director of the Nobel Institute for Physical Chemistry near Stockholm. He remained there until his death on October 2, 1927.

ent gases experimentally, Tyndall built the first ratio *spectrophotometer*, a device that measures light intensity. He was amazed at the abilities of colorless and invisible gases and vapors to absorb and transmit radiant heat. His experiments demonstrated that nitrogen (which makes up 78 percent of the Earth's atmosphere), oxygen (which makes up 21 percent of the Earth's atmosphere), and hydrogen were virtually transparent to radiant heat, meaning the most abundant components of the atmosphere did not affect the transmission of heat. More minor components, water vapor, carbon dioxide, and *ozone*, absorbed heat efficiently. He found that absorption and radiation properties of vapors followed the same order in the corresponding liquids. This was important because these properties could not be studied directly for water vapor since it condensed. He discovered that water vapor was the strongest heat absorber, acting like a blanket over the Earth, and therefore had the greatest effect on the Earth's surface temperature. He estimated that a single molecule of water vapor absorbed and radiated 16,000 times more than one molecule of air. Without the aqueous vapor, he predicted destruction of the Earth's plant life from frost.

Tyndall explained the formation of dew and hoarfrost as being caused by a loss of heat through radiation. In "On the Passage of Radiant Heat through Dry and Humid Air," published in *Philosophical Magazine* in 1863, he wisely stated that the role of water vapor "must form one of the chief foundation stones of the science of meteorology." He suspected that changes in the levels of water vapor and carbon dioxide in the atmosphere accounted for the changes in historical climate revealed by geological research.

This research suggested the existence of a greenhouse effect in the atmosphere. In a greenhouse, short wavelength solar radiation enters easily through a slanted glass roof, some of the energy is absorbed, and the emitted infrared radiation (with longer wavelengths) is trapped inside by the walls and the roof. When radiant heat from the Sun enters into the atmosphere, some is immediately reflected back into space by the atmosphere and clouds, and the rest warms the land and the seas. Some of the warmth is returned to space in the form of infrared rays, but when the rays encounter absorptive gases such as water vapor and carbon dioxide, their journey back into space is disrupted. The gases radiate some heat back into space as infrared rays, and the remainder returns to the Earth's surface as heat. Other scientists had predicted this greenhouse phenomenon, but Tyndall was the first to provide experimental verification for it.

Why the Sky Is Blue

In 1869, Tyndall observed that when a beam of light passes through a colloidal solution, a solution containing tiny particles, the light is scattered in several different directions by the particles, allowing it to be viewed from the side. When passing through pure, highly filtered water, a beam of light cannot be observed from the side. Similar results occurred when using filtered or unfiltered air as the medium. He concluded that light was only visible when it reflected

TYNDALL EFFECT

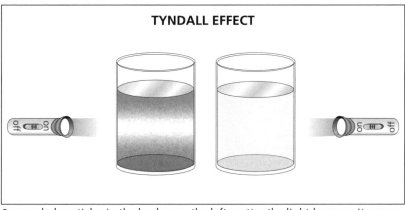

Suspended particles in the beaker on the left scatter the light beam as it passes through the solution, making it visible from the side.

off particles in the air or in the water, a phenomenon now called the Tyndall effect.

Tyndall continued these studies by examining the effects of colloidal solutions on different wavelengths of light and found that the size of the particles affected the way the light was scattered. Shorter wavelengths of light (violet) scattered more than longer wavelengths of light (red). The English physicist Lord Rayleigh later figured out that light was scattered with an efficiency inversely proportional to the fourth power of the wavelength. In 1869, the Royal Society awarded Tyndall the Rumford Medal for this research. Tyndall applied this new knowledge to determine levels of pollution in the London atmosphere by measuring the amount of light scattered by particles in the air.

The Tyndall effect explains the blue color of the sky. The Earth's atmosphere is a colloid containing dust, molecules, and other particulate matter that scatter the sunlight. The reason one can still see while in a shadow is due to this dispersion. Because the particles of dust in the atmosphere are extremely tiny, they interfere with short wavelengths more than larger wavelengths. Because of this, they scatter the blue light waves the best, making the sky appear blue on a clear day. During times when the sunlight must penetrate thicker lengths of atmosphere to reach the Earth's surface, such as dusk, much of the blue light has been removed by scattering. The sunset

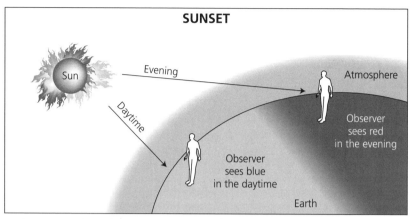

As the sun sets, its radiation must penetrate longer lengths of atmosphere to reach the Earth's surface, making the sky appear reddish orange rather than blue.

appears reddish-orange because only light of those longer wavelengths reaches the Earth's surface unaffected.

Foghorns

After Faraday died in 1866, Tyndall succeeded him as scientific advisor to the Trinity House and Board of Trade. His responsibility was to oversee and improve upon the safety and welfare of seafarers. In this capacity, Tyndall examined the transmission of light and sound through air in connection with lighthouse and siren work. Understanding how sounds traveled through air would help in making better foghorns for use by ships. Tyndall discovered that variations in the amount of water vapor present or in the temperature affected the sound waves traveling through the atmosphere, so sometimes different wavelengths were transmitted differently. Even visually clear air may contain clouds that obstruct the transmission of sound. He recommended the steam siren as the most powerful. Tyndall also studied and reported on the gas system used to illuminate lighthouses until he resigned from his post in 1883.

The Defeat of Spontaneous Generation

In the 19th century, the cause of food spoilage still baffled scientists. Some believed that the appearance of maggots on exposed meat and the contamination of heat-sterilized liquid broths demonstrated that life arose from nonliving matter, a theory called *spontaneous generation* or abiogenesis. The repeated contamination of heated broths dumbfounded biologists and prevented many of them from dismissing the theory of spontaneous generation. During the 1860s, French scientist Louis Pasteur was working to elucidate the role of microorganisms in the spoilage of wine during fermentation, and he showed that keeping dust out of broths prevented their contamination. Tyndall admired Pasteur, and during the 1870s, he investigated the cause of food spoilage with Pasteur's experiments in mind. Tyndall prevented putrefaction of dead fish and meat by exposing them only to highly-filtered pure air, demonstrating that germ-free air was incapable of developing bacterial life and causing food spoilage. The same dust particles that Tyndall had previously shown to scatter light also carried microscopic organisms that spoiled food. Air through which a beam of light could be observed must have in it tiny dust particles causing the light to scatter. Such air was not optically pure and led to bacterial growth.

Tyndall went further to show that intermittent heating was more effective for sterilizing solutions than simple boiling. The first increase in temperature killed live bacteria, but dormant bacterial spores were not destroyed. The description of the sterilization technique by discontinuous heating, called *Tyndallization*, advanced food preservation methodology.

Popularization of Natural Philosophy

Tyndall was as famous for his popularization of science as he was for his scientific contributions. He wrote articles in magazines promoting science to the general public and several books summarizing the current state of knowledge in different subfields of science. Tyndall published popular physics books on heat, light, sound, electricity, ice, water, vapor, and air, most running multiple editions. During 1872 and 1873, Tyndall made a round of lectures in the United States that earned him a substantial amount in fees. In a gesture typical of his noble nature, he donated the entire amount for the development of the sciences in America. Another memorable act was Tyndall's inaugural presidential address to the British Association in 1874 in Belfast. He promoted experiment and verification in the search of truth and opposed what he called the anti-scientific tenet of Christianity, including prayer, miracles, and a creative power. In response to the Belfast address, churches around the world denounced Tyndall for blasphemy.

Tyndall made other contributions to science, including making the first light pipe in 1854, leading to today's fiber optics. He devised a fireman's helmet respirator that consisted of layers of cotton-wool and charcoal to absorb contaminants. He also invented an artificial sky and sunset using photochemical reactions. During his 33-year tenure at the Royal Institution, Tyndall also served as an examiner for the Royal Military College and as professor of physics at the Royal School of Mines as well as lecturing all over to scientists and the general public.

In 1876, at the age of 56, Tyndall had married Louisa Hamilton. They never had children but remained married until Tyndall's death. After 1885, they spent most of their time at a house they purchased on Hindhead, Surrey, England. In 1887, Tyndall retired as superintendent of the Royal Institution due to his failing health. Prolonged, persistent insomnia led to his eventual accidental overdose of a sleeping drug, chloral, administered by his wife. Tyndall passed away on December 4, 1893, at 73 years of age.

During his lifetime, Tyndall published an impressive 16 books and 180 experimental papers over a wide range of scientific topics. He was the recipient of five honorary doctorates and belonged to 35 scientific societies. He made significant contributions to bacteriology and maritime navigation, and his research on diamagnetism and mechanical pressure still is relevant in solid state and applied physics. His studies on the transmission and absorption of radiant heat and the profound influence of atmospheric water vapor on temperature and climate had a direct impact on meteorology. Though most historical accounts of Tyndall's life emphasize his contributions as a lecturer and a promoter of science, he also earned remembrance as a pioneer of atmospheric and climatic research.

CHRONOLOGY

1820	John Tyndall is born on August 2 at Leighlinbridge, County Carlow, Ireland
1839–42	Works for the Irish Ordnance Survey as surveyor and draftsman
1842–43	Works for the English Survey
1844–47	Participates in the construction of the United Kingdom railway network
1847	Teaches mathematics at Queenwood College, Hampshire
1848	Enters the University of Marburg in Germany
1850	Earns a doctorate degree in mathematics from the University of Marburg and begins studies on diamagnetism and magnetic optical properties of crystals
1851–53	Returns to Queenwood College as a lecturer in mathematics and natural philosophy
1853	Accepts position as a professor of natural philosophy at the Royal Institution
1857–60	Studies glacier motion
1859–70	Studies radiant heat and atmospheric gases
1866–83	Serves as scientific advisor to Trinity House, overseeing safety measures for marine navigation
1867	Succeeds Faraday as superintendent of the Royal Institution and begins studying sound
1868–71	Studies diffusion of light in the atmosphere
1869	Describes the Tyndall effect, the diffusion of light by large molecules and dust. Explains why the sky is blue
1870–81	Studies spontaneous generation and sterilization techniques. Shows food decay only occurs in air that is not optically pure, evidence against the theory of spontaneous generation

| 1887 | Retires from Royal Institution, becomes an honorary pro-fessor |
| 1893 | Dies on December 4 at Hindhead, Surrey, England, from an accidental overdose of chloral administered by his wife |

FURTHER READING

Earth Observatory, National Aeronautics and Space Administration. "On the Shoulders of Giants: John Tyndall (1820–1893)." Available online. URL: http://earthobservatory.nasa.gov/Library/Giants/Tyndall. Accessed February 8, 2005. Biographical profile of Tyndall with links to biographies of other scientists who have made contributions to the understanding of the Earth's climate and environmental changes.

Fleming, James Rodger. *Historical Perspectives on Climate Change.* New York: Oxford University Press, 1998. Contains a chapter on the contributions of Tyndall and Svante August Arrhenius and the early research on carbon dioxide and climate.

Gillispie, Charles C., ed. *Dictionary of Scientific Biography.* Vol. 13. New York: Scribner, 1970–76. Good source for facts concerning personal background and scientific accomplishments but assumes reader has basic knowledge of science.

Stephen, Leslie, and Sidney Lee, eds. *The Dictionary of National Biography.* Vol. 19. London: Oxford University Press, 1921–22. Brief account of lives and works of famous people from Great Britain in encyclopedia format.

Tyndall Centre for Climate Change Research. "Who Was John Tyndall?" Available online. URL: http://www.tyndall.ac.uk/general/john_tyndall.shtml. Last modified October 26, 2001. Information on the man for whom the center is named with links to a biography and a summary of his research on gases and climate.

Cleveland Abbe

(1838–1916)

Cleveland Abbe instituted daily weather reporting for the general public and was instrumental in the creation of the National Weather Service. *(Courtesy of the National Oceanic and Atmospheric Administration/Department of Commerce)*

America's First Weatherman

On the front page of almost every newspaper in the United States, a short blurb foretells the day's weather, and inside its pages one can find a more complete account of expected temperatures and rainfall for the upcoming week. Agricultural procedures and military maneuvers as well as sporting events and family picnics all depend on what the National Weather Service predicts nature will bring. Though meteorologists were already mapping current conditions and farmers and naval navigation offices collected almanacs of weather related data, the first daily bulletin forecasting local weather did not appear until 1869. The phenomenon was the brainchild of Professor Cleveland Abbe, nicknamed "America's First Weatherman" and "Old Probabilities." Abbe was a meteorologist who dedicated his life to advancing knowledge in the meteorological and climatological sciences and to establishing a network of weather reporting services.

Dreams of Astronomy

Cleveland Abbe was born on December 3, 1838, in New York, New York, to Charlotte Colgate and George Waldo Abbe, a charitable dry goods businessman who helped found the American Bible Union. Cleveland entered public school at age 12 and became interested in meteorology after watching a teacher perform experiments on electricity and thunderstorms. In 1851, he enrolled at the New York Free Academy (now the City College of New York), where learning mathematics, chemistry, and physics incited an interest in science. He enjoyed studying the stars from his rooftop using the school's telescope, and when the smoke and heat in the city sky interfered with his viewing, he lugged the scope to his grandfather's farm in Windham, Connecticut.

After receiving a bachelor of arts degree in 1857, Abbe taught mathematics at Trinity Grammar School to earn money while continuing his studies toward a master of arts degree, which he completed in 1860. Abbe's father wanted him to become a mathematics teacher, but by then Abbe had decided to become an astronomer. From 1859 to 1860, he studied astronomy at the University of Michigan while teaching civil engineering at the Michigan Agricultural College (now Michigan State University) and the University of Michigan.

From 1860 to 1864, Abbe performed his first astronomical work computing telegraphic longitudes for the U.S. Coast Survey at the Harvard Observatory. While at Cambridge, Massachusetts, he took courses at the Harvard Graduate School taught by the famous naturalist Louis Agassiz, whose research on glaciers supported the existence of a historical ice age. Abbe tried to join the military when the

Civil War broke out in 1861, but severe nearsightedness prevented him from enlisting. In 1864, the British Natural History Society elected him to membership.

From Russia to Washington

Abbe headed for Pulkova, Russia, in December 1864, to study astronomy at the Nicholas Central Observatory. Pulkova was a small, cold, serf village with not even a store or a post office; there was nothing to distract him from studying astronomy and learning how to use the special instruments. Though life may have been monotonous, Abbe felt all he was learning there would help him advance American astronomy when he returned to the United States. Letters he wrote home indicated his desire to have his own observatory. He originally planned to stay at the Pulkova Observatory for several years, but he returned home near the end of 1866 after a love affair soured.

While seeking a directorship for an observatory, Abbe temporarily worked with the U.S. Naval Observatory. The Cincinnati Observatory in Ohio, which had the sixth-largest telescope in existence, offered Abbe a job in 1868, and he took charge that June. The observatory had not had a director since 1859 and was not only in a terrible state of disrepair, but also had been omitted from the list of principal observatories of the world that was printed annually in the national *Nautical Almanac and Astronomical Ephemeris.*

The Daily Weather Bulletin

Abbe spent the first several weeks organizing major repairs, such as fixing leaks in the roof and broken windows. Even after restoring the building to a satisfactory physical condition, a lot of money would have been necessary to renovate it and purchase equipment for modern astronomical research. Even if such funds had been available, the building's location itself was unsatisfactory, as it was in the middle of a smoke-saturated city, obstructing celestial observations. In his inaugural report to the board of control, Abbe recommended switching the focus of the observatory from astronomy to meteorology, which would require minimal financial support, be useful to the citizens, be more profitable, and would improve the reputation of the observatory. Abbe had been interested in meteorology, particularly since reading the classic article, "The Motions of Fluids and Solids Relative to the Earth's Surface," by William Ferrel in *Mathematical Monthly* (published in parts in 1859–60). Ferrel's landmark article that mathematically explained the general circulation of the atmosphere, including the significant effect of the Earth's rotation, gave Abbe confidence that scientists could uncover the complex mechanisms of the atmosphere.

The summary of plans Abbe submitted to the board included compiling a daily bulletin of telegraph dispatches from meteorological observers across the country. This data would aid in the prediction of weather that potentially could destroy crops or cause terrible shipwrecks. Except for making a planned expedition to the Dakotas to observe a total eclipse of the Sun on August 7, 1869, Abbe busied himself preparing the long-deserted observatory for his meteorological plans. He set up loaned and donated instruments and made important contacts at newspapers and local colleges and schools. He started collecting books and organized the Meteorological Union for the Ohio Valley.

Abbe wanted to anticipate the weather by one day. Meteorologists knew that storms moved eastward over the nation, temperature and humidity increased and the air pressure decreased as a storm approached, winds blew toward the storm center, and how to calculate speeds. In combination with information about the weather conditions at various locations in the country, this knowledge would allow one to know if a storm was coming, when it would arrive, and how dangerous it was. Just a few hours notice could potentially save lives and valuable property.

September 1, 1869, was the anticipated date for meteorological observers from 14 stations to send telegraph reports on the local weather conditions, including barometer readings, temperature, humidity, direction and force of wind, types of clouds and direction of their motion, amount of rain or snow, and general conditions of the atmosphere. Though only two of the promised reports arrived on time with one more arriving later in the day, Abbe remained characteristically optimistic. He manually wrote the *Daily Weather Bulletin* the first week. Within a week, a few more of the voluntary

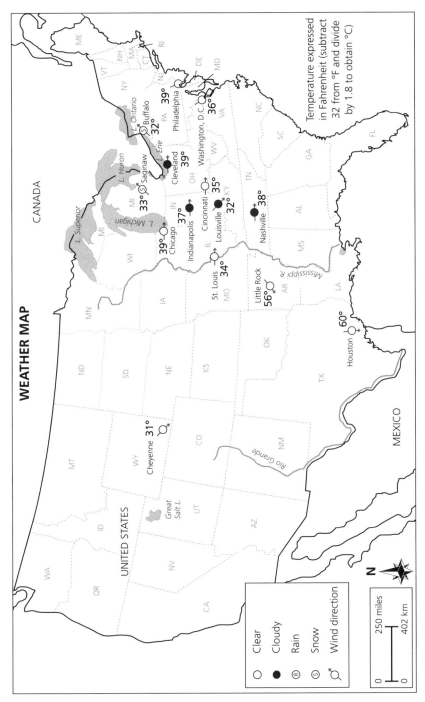

Abbe's daily weather maps clearly provided basic information on temperature, precipitation, and wind from cities across the nation.

observers began sending reports, and the first printed bulletin was posted on the Cincinnati Chamber of Commerce bulletin board on September 8, 1869. The chamber supported the project for three months, during which time up to 22 stations began sending regular reports, and interested parties initiated subscriptions. Abbe solicited support from the Western Union Telegraph Company for free telegrams twice daily and asked the press to defray costs since the weather bulletin was copied into the city's papers.

By the first of December, the observatory no longer printed the *Daily Weather Bulletin* independently, but it continued to appear in the morning papers. The weather report had improved over time and now included information concerning wind and temperatures compiled from 33 stations, including Boston, New Orleans, Charleston, and Milwaukee. Western Union Telegraph Company undertook the responsibility of compiling the daily reports and charts for the newspapers. On February 22, 1870, Abbe published the first daily weather map for the general public. On the map, Abbe circled the reporting cities and used basic symbols to represent precipitation, wind direction, and temperatures.

Creation of a National Weather Service

The reports in Cincinnati were particularly useful to farmers, who benefited from knowing when to expect frosts and the anticipated temperatures each day, but such information could also have been useful in preventing marine disasters. In 1869, the United States suffered 1,914 marine casualties, including 209 lost lives and over $4 million in lost property. Abbe's daily weather bulletins proved so useful that, on February 9, 1870, the government passed a National Weather Service Bill that provided for the establishment of a national weather observation system under the direction of the Signal Corps for the Army. The newly proposed weather service was responsible for collecting meteorological information from military stations across the continent and giving notice on the Atlantic seaboard and northern lakes of the approach and force of storms by telegraphs.

Though the bill passed in record time, less than two months from submission of the original proposal to obtaining the presidential signature, the Signal Corps was not immediately ready to take on the new responsibility of forecasting. In January 1871, the chief signal officer, General Albert Myer, appointed Abbe, the only man with experience forecasting the weather for the use of the public, as civilian assistant. With expert knowledge and extreme patience, Abbe created what became the Weather Bureau, now the National Weather Service. Aware that little was known about meteorological forecasting, he pushed the War Department for funding to support systematic theoretical and experimental studies. He faced a lot of opposition, but he was persistent and fought for what he felt was important. The Signal Corps began enlisting college graduates who were more suitable for meteorological work and relieved them of ordinary duties. They also established a study room, where Abbe and other professors taught courses and tackled problems with the assistance of other meteorologists. The military did not appreciate that success in scientific research did not necessarily follow set deadline schedules or thrive under the demand for specific written work orders, but Abbe defended the scientific work of the Weather Bureau. On July 1, 1891, Congress transferred the weather service from the Signal Corps of the War Department to a special department of its own in the Department of Agriculture, appointing Abbe professor of meteorology.

A Matter of Time

Abbe promoted a nationally established system of standards for thermometers, barometers, and other weights and measures that grew into the Bureau of Standards, but he was also influential in the establishment of standard time. In 1868, Abbe supplied the City of Cincinnati with the correct time. The observatories that supplied him with local weather conditions also had to supply the correct time, but the fact that each city had its own time complicated matters. He recognized the problems this also caused with railroad travel, time of telegraph dispatches, and public convenience and wanted Congress to pass a law standardizing time across the nation. He asked F. A. P. Barnard, the president of the American Meteorological Society, for assistance in engaging public interest in this subject, and in turn, Barnard appointed Abbe chair of a special committee on standard time.

In 1879, Abbe submitted a report proposing standard time with hourly differences based on Greenwich as the starting point. The

Time Measurement

Reporting the correct time was crucial for Cleveland Abbe's weather forecasts so he could estimate when an oncoming storm might arrive, the number of hours of daylight, or what time the frost on a crop may melt. In trying to establish standard time across the nation, Abbe taught observatories in other cities how to determine the correct time. How is time determined and measured? The ancient Babylonians divided days into 24-hour periods giving 12 hours to daylight and 12 hours to darkness. They also divided a circle into 360 degrees, and later each degree was partitioned into 60 minutes. Clockmakers followed suit and divided each minute into 60 seconds.

The *celestial meridian* is an imaginary curved line that passes through the sky and helps people measure time using the Sun. As the Earth rotates about its axis, the time when the Sun crosses over the celestial meridian (once each day) for a particular location is designated noon. Midnight occurs by definition 12 hours later. To complicate matters, this means of measuring time results in varying day lengths due to the tilt of the Earth, the oval shape of its orbit, and the speed as it orbits the Sun, thus astronomers adjust for this by using an imaginary mean or average Sun.

Sidereal time is time measured by the apparent motion of the fixed stars as the Earth moves. A sidereal day is approximately four minutes shorter than a solar day, as determined above. One can also use the regular appearance of the full Moon, occurring every 29.5 days, to measure time.

Royal Observatory in Greenwich, England, is positioned on the *prime meridian,* an imaginary line running north-south, designated zero degrees longitude. He suggested that every 15 degrees westward represent a time lag of one hour, since there are 24 hours in a day and 360 degrees circling the globe (24 × 15 = 360). Abbe also published a letter to the editor of the *New York Tribune* advocating such a reform. In 1880, Sanford Fleming, chief engineer of the Canadian Pacific Railway, wrote Abbe asking permission to use the report that he wrote as chairman of the committee on standard time for the American Meteorological Society. Abbe graciously allowed Fleming to use the report and an accompanying letter as he saw fit. In October 1884, an international agreement adopted the Greenwich meridian as the basis for standard hourly time.

A Useful Servant

In 1873, Abbe founded the *Monthly Weather Review* (published by the U.S. Weather Bureau), now a leading meteorological journal of the American Meteorological Society, and he served as editor from 1893 to 1916. The journal included charts, diagrams, and tables compiled from weather data from more than 3,000 weather stations. His knowledge about meteorology was vast, and he was responsible for ensuring the articles were scientifically accurate, complete, and sound.

Abbe thought it was important to provide opportunities for others to learn about meteorology; he lectured publicly, at Columbian College (now George Washington University), and at Johns Hopkins University. He also helped found the Washington Philosophical Society and was a very early member of the National Geographic Society and the Washington Anthropological Society. He wrote prolifically about meteorological instruments, methods, standards for thermometers and barometers, actinometry, climate, long-range weather predictions, and biographies of famous meteorologists.

Interested in the upper atmosphere, Abbe started using kites to study winds in 1867. He encouraged the Signal Corps to make balloon ascents solely for meteorological observations in 1872. In the 1890s, Abbe systematically studied kite flying for the Weather Bureau. He helped develop the best form for kites equipped with instruments to collect meteorological data such as temperature, air pressure, humidity, and wind velocity. With Abbe's assistance, the bureau established 17 kite-flying stations around the Great Lakes, upper Mississippi, and the upper Missouri valleys. Using information gathered during 1,217 kite flights between May and October 1898, he was able to establish parameters for normal air conditions. The Weather Bureau reached the amazing altitude of 23,110 feet (over 7,000 m) above sea level using eight kites in tandem from the Mount Weather Station in 1907.

Shortly after starting work as director of the Cincinnati Observatory, Abbe hired Frances Martha Neal as his secretary. She was helpful in copying his notes and letters, appreciated science and scholarship, and was devoted to charities. Abbe married her on May 10, 1870, and they had three sons together. Martha Abbe was diagnosed with diabetes in 1903 and died from the disease in 1908. The following year, at age 70, Abbe married Margaret Augusta Percival, who cared for him until his death on October 28, 1916, in Chevy Chase, Maryland, from complications of skin cancer. He was buried in the Rock Creek Cemetery in Washington, D.C. The flags at the Weather Bureau were flown at half-mast on November 3, 1916, in his honor.

Abbe had been a member of at least 39 scientific and learned societies, received several honorary degrees, and wrote 290 papers, but he was best remembered by his friends and colleagues for his amicable personality and willingness to always help others. He generously donated hundreds of books to the Washington Public Library and much of his private library to Johns Hopkins University. In 1906, the American Philosophical Society awarded him the Franklin Medal, and in 1912, the Royal Meteorological Society presented him with their highest meteorological honor, the Symons Memorial Gold Medal. The National Academy of Sciences decorated Abbe with the Marcellus Hartley Gold Medal for eminence in the application of science to the public welfare in 1916. That same year, the new Weather Bureau building in Cincinnati was dedicated to him and named the Abbe Meteorological Observatory. Today the American Meteorological Society honors Abbe by presenting the Cleveland Abbe Award to distinguished individuals who have served the atmospheric sciences.

The nation is now dependent on the result of Abbe's labors. His initial efforts to provide a local weather forecast in a daily newspaper found him struggling to convince voluntary observers to send him telegraphs of local weather reports. The success of the daily weather reports and his optimistic persistence led to an act of Congress that established the National Weather Service, the most important weather reporting organization in the world. Not only did Abbe institute weather forecasting, but he actively promoted standard time and meteorological education, pioneered weather map analysis, and served as editor for scholarly journals and several encyclopedias. Thomas Corwin Mendenhall, a professor who organized the Ohio Weather Bureau, composed the following words that are found in Humphrey's memorial biography of Abbe written for the National Academy of Sciences:

"When one considers the small beginning in 1869 at the Cincinnati Observatory, with a few daily telegrams generously donated by the Western Union Telegraph Company, a local forecast printed in a single daily newspaper, and then turns to the present splendid organization, with its thousands of observers, its two or more daily forecasts printed in every city and town, and reaching by telephone or otherwise the remotest corners of the country, its storm warnings, its frost and flood warnings by which annually property worth many millions of dollars is saved from destruction, its important investigations in the field of agricultural meteorology and its other useful functions, one cannot avoid the conclusion that the nation has had few more useful servants than Cleveland Abbe."

CHRONOLOGY

1838	Cleveland Abbe is born on December 3 in New York, New York
1857	Receives a bachelor of arts degree from the New York Free Academy (now the City College of New York)
1857–58	Tutors in mathematics at Trinity Grammar School in New York

1859–60	Teaches engineering at Michigan Agricultural College (now Michigan State University) and the University of Michigan while studying astronomy at the University of Michigan
1860	Receives a master of arts degree from the New York Free Academy
1860–64	Performs telegraphic longitude work in Cambridge, Massachusetts
1865–66	Works at the Nicholas Central Observatory in Pulkova, Russia
1867	Accepts position of aid in the U.S. Naval Observatory
1868	Becomes director of the Cincinnati Observatory
1869	Starts *Daily Weather Bulletin*
1871–91	The U.S. Army employs Abbe as professor of meteorology and civilian assistant in the Office of the Chief Signal Officer in Washington, D.C.
1884	Becomes professor of meteorology at Columbian University (now George Washington University)
1891–1916	The U.S. Weather Bureau of the Department of Agriculture employs Abbe as professor of meteorology
1896	Begins lecturing on meteorology at Johns Hopkins University
1916	Retires due to poor health
1916	Dies on October 28 from skin cancer in Chevy Chase, Maryland

FURTHER READING

Abbe, Truman. *Professor Abbe and the Isobars: The Story of Cleveland Abbe, America's First Weatherman.* New York: Vantage Press, 1955. A biography written by Abbe's son based on Abbe's papers and correspondence.

Biographical Memoirs. National Academy of Sciences. Vol. 8. Washington, D.C.: National Academy of Sciences, 1919. Fullest memoir of Abbe, written by a distinguished colleague for the premier scientific organization of the United States.

Cox, John D. *Storm Watchers: The Turbulent History of Weather Prediction from Franklin's Kite to El Niño.* Hoboken, N.J.: John Wiley, 2002. Highlights the work of early weathermen and outlines the evolution of weather forecasting.

Garraty, John A., and Mark C. Carnes, eds. *American National Biography.* Vol. 1. New York: Oxford University Press, 1999. Brief account of lives and works of famous Americans in encyclopedia format.

Humphreys, W. J. "Giants of Science: Cleveland Abbe," Available online. URL: http://www.history.noaa.gov/giants/abbe.html. Last updated May 12, 2004. Lots of biographical information as well as links to the "NOAA Legacy: History of the Weather Service" and Abbe's description of the signal service.

Vilhelm Bjerknes

(1862–1951)

Vilhelm Bjerknes is considered the father of modern meteorology. (*Science Photo Library/Photo Researchers, Inc.*)

The Movement of Air Masses in the Atmosphere

Discussions about daily weather have occurred at breakfast tables for thousands of years but did not enter academic lecture halls or university research labs until the 20th century. Vilhelm Bjerknes was a Norwegian physicist who researched the movement of air and improved the accuracy of weather forecasting. His application of hydrodynamics and *thermodynamics* to the descriptive subject of weather transformed it into the scientific field of meteorology by explaining the behavior of air masses at *fronts* where different masses met. Under his leadership, Bergen, Norway, became an influential center for meteorological research that spawned a model for the evolution of a cyclone. The results of his research form the foundation of theoretical and practical atmospheric sciences, earning him the title of father of modern meteorology.

A Father's Influence

Vilhelm Friman Koren Bjerknes (pronounced BYERK-nays) was born on March 14, 1862, in Christiania (renamed Oslo in 1925), Norway, to Carl A. Bjerknes and Aletta Koren. The senior Bjerknes was a mathematician and physicist who conducted investigations in electromagnetism and the transmission of forces through fluids. In 1880, Vilhelm entered the University of Kristiania (formerly known as the University of Christiania and now the University of Oslo) to study mathematics and physics, which he applied to research he performed in collaboration with his father. In 1887, Vilhelm ventured out on his own and began work toward a master's degree.

After obtaining a master of science degree in 1888, Vilhelm received a state fellowship to travel to Paris, where he attended lectures given by French mathematician Henri Poincaré on *electrodynamics*, the study of electrical currents. From there he moved to Bonn, Germany, and became an assistant to Heinrich Hertz, the German physicist who had recently demonstrated the existence of electromagnetic waves, as predicted by British physicist James Clerk Maxwell in the mid-19th century. This discovery forced Vilhelm's father to abandon his studies on the action of electromagnetic forces at a distance, since they did not act at a distance at all but instead traveled from one point in a medium to another point as waves. Studies on electrical resonance carried out by Vilhelm and Hertz were essential to the development of wireless radio communication. Bjerknes returned to Norway to further his education, earning a doctorate degree in physics from the University of Kristiania in 1892. The following year, Stockholm's School of Mining hired him as a lecturer in applied mechanics, and he accepted an appointment as professor of applied mechanics and mathematical physics at the University of Stockholm in 1895.

In 1895, Bjerknes married Honoria Bonnevie, with whom he had four sons. Their second oldest, Jacob, was destined to follow in his father's footsteps by becoming a respected meteorologist.

Physical Hydrodynamics

Shortly after arriving in Stockholm, Bjerknes focused his research on hydrodynamics, the science of the motion of fluids and the forces exerted by fluids, studies that he had initiated under his father's tutelage. He translated his new expertise on the transmission of electromagnetic forces by the propagation of waves, disturbances that transfer energy from one point to another through a medium, to the field of hydrodynamics. What produced motion within a fluid, and what was the mechanical basis for the transmission of forces across distances within fluids? He imagined a body of fluid surrounded by fluid of a different density. Classical theory explained the distribution of different densities in a fluid system due to differences in pressure, but Bjerknes's investigations suggested this resulted in the production of *vortices*, circular motions of fluid, at the boundaries between the inner fluid body and the surrounding medium. His conclusion contradicted accepted theorems that stated such motions were conserved in compressible fluids—they were not created nor did they fade away. Careful consideration led Bjerknes to realize that classical theory explaining fluid dynamics accounted for the density distribution in a fluid due to differences in pressure, but differences in temperature and composition also affected the density distribution in heterogeneous fluids. Following this epiphany in 1897, he derived a set of new circulation theorems by generalizing the existing theorems to include thermodynamic (heat-related) factors.

The usefulness of this theory of physical hydrodynamics lay in Bjerknes's application of these mathematical equations to the world's largest fluid systems—the oceans and the atmosphere. In the oceans, temperature and salinity affect densities, and in the atmosphere, temperature and humidity do the same, giving rise to movement. Surprisingly, thermal energy had never been related to the circulation of the atmosphere. Because air was simply a mixture of gases in the atmosphere, natural physical laws dictated its behavior, and the application of principles of thermodynamics, the study of heat, explained its motion. Heat energy from the Sun caused molecules in the Earth's atmosphere to move, and motion of those molecules resulted in friction from rubbing up against one another. The friction produced additional heat, which converted into more movement. Bjerknes's circulation theorems mathematically described what happened to a fluid when its temperature changed. As air warmed, it became lighter and rose, and as air cooled, it became heavier and sunk.

An Ambitious Program

In 1904, Bjerknes presented a lecture titled "A Rational Method for Weather Prediction" to the Stockholm Physics Society. He proposed a program for developing numerical weather prediction based on applying mathematical equations to information from initial atmospheric conditions. Because movement of air in the atmosphere was the source of weather patterns, combining knowledge of thermodynamics with principles of hydrodynamics would allow more accurate weather forecasting. Current atmospheric conditions were the consequence of natural forces acting on the preceding atmospheric conditions; therefore, applying physical principles to known initial atmospheric conditions would allow one to predict accurate future conditions. Bjerknes's ideas were unique because instead of simply offering a physical description of fluids, he applied physical principles to the development, progression, and demise of specific weather phenomena. This scientific backing lent credibility to weather prediction and increased its accuracy. He traveled to the United States in 1905, seeking funding to advance the methods of his meteorological program. The Carnegie Institution in Washington, D.C., was impressed and awarded him an annual grant for his ambitious, farsighted research program for 36 years.

In 1907, the University of Kristiania appointed Bjerknes professor of applied mechanics and mathematical physics. His research goal was to develop new approaches for applying physical mechanics to atmospheric and oceanic circulation, but he needed a lot of data to show others how to apply his methods and to convince others of the usefulness of these new methods. He spent a lot of energy during his first few years at Kristiania convincing his peers of the need for international cooperation in standardizing units and data gathering to accomplish what he called "a conquest of the air by science." He wrote the first volume of a series explaining his ideas, *Dynamic Meteorology and Hydrography* (1910) with Johann Wilhelm Sandström, describing the resting conditions of the atmosphere and oceans. The following year he published the second volume, dealing with *kinematics*, the study of pure motions without reference to the mass or force of the objects, with two assistants, Theodor Hesselberg and Olav M. Devik. A third volume, written by his collaborators, was published in 1951. The volumes were well received, and over time, meteorologists implemented the suggestions for improvements to weather analysis.

Bjerknes eventually became frustrated by the lack of space and resources in Kristiania. He accepted a professorship in geophysics at the University of Leipzig, Germany, and upon arriving in 1913, established its new geophysical institute, the first academic training and research center devoted specifically to atmospheric science. *Lines of convergence*, where wind from two different directions comes together, became one of the major research focal points in Leipzig. Bjerknes's group looked for a relationship between lines of convergence and *line squalls*, rapidly moving bands of thunderstorms accompanied by powerful winds. During his tenure at Leipzig, Bjerknes's reputation grew, but the onset of World War I in 1914 hindered research efforts. When Norwegian oceanographer and polar explorer Fridtjof Nansen arranged the opportunity for Bjerknes to establish a new geophysical institute in Bergen, Bjerknes gratefully accepted, and he moved back to Norway during the summer of 1917.

Battle in the Atmosphere

Bjerknes founded the Geophysics Institute as part of the Bergen Museum in 1917. (The Bergen Museum expanded to become the University of Bergen in 1948.) As a seaport, the location was ideal

Jacob Bjerknes

Though Vilhelm Bjerknes introduced his son Jacob (Jack) to meteorology, Jack, born on November 2, 1897, earned his own reputation as an esteemed leader in the field. Meteorologists have attributed the many accomplishments of the father and son to their ability to work as a unit, complementing one another.

Jack started assisting his father in Leipzig in 1917, but that same year the family moved to Bergen, where in 1918, Jack became the chief forecaster of the Bergen weather service. One of Jack's major contributions to meteorology was the introduction of rational methods for weather prediction, which resulted from his analysis of lines of convergence and their connection with other weather phenomena such as line squalls. He observed that in the Northern Hemisphere, a line of convergence moved to the right of someone looking along the line in the direction of the wind converging toward it. He also described two distinct rain patterns associated with lines of convergence—a wide, band-shaped rain area and a narrow line squall. With knowledge about weather and wind conditions nearby, the Bergen group hoped to use Jack's findings to predict rain several hours in advance, information that would be valuable to farmers.

Though the calculations did not prove useful, the studies led to his conclusion that moving cyclones, or *midlatitude* low pressure systems, contained two lines of convergence. Counterclockwise circular and upward moving warm masses were flanked by colder air on two sides, with defined boundaries that were often associated with the leading edge of a storm. In 1918, at the young age of 20, he published "On the Structure of Moving Cyclones" in *Geofysiske publikasjoner*, and over the next several years, these ideas evolved into the polar front theory of midlatitude cyclones.

Jack Bjerknes became professor of meteorology at the Bergen Museum in 1931. While he was visiting the United States in 1940, the Germans invaded Norway, and he could not return home. The University of California at Los Angeles appointed him professor of meteorology and head of the section of meteorology in the department of physics. Five years later, he established and served as chair of the department of meteorology, which grew rapidly and became a world-class center for teaching and research in atmospheric science.

In the 1930s, Jack had further developed his ideas about cyclonic and anticyclonic (high pressure systems) activity to include upper air currents. This paved the way for his research on the newly discovered *jet stream* in the 1950s. Jet streams are currents of wind in the upper atmosphere that travel very fast, averaging around 110 miles (180 km) per hour in the winter and approximately half that in the summer, and they are often associated with storms or tornadoes.

In 1969, Jack proposed a positive feedback interaction between the oceanic temperature and the atmosphere, referred to as the Bjerknes hypothesis. He suggested that warming of the sea surface temperatures off the west coast of South America weakened the *trade winds* blowing toward the equator traveling from the northeast or southeast. The weaker winds reduced the upwelling of colder subsurface waters, a process that normally acts to cool the surface waters. This leads to further warming of the sea surface waters, continuing the positive feedback loop. This cyclical warming phenomenon of the east Pacific Ocean is called El Niño, and it significantly affects weather patterns in and around the United States.

Jack Bjerknes received the U.S. National Medal of Science from Lyndon Johnson in 1966. The citation read, "By watching and studying maps, he discovered the cyclone-making waves of the air and the climate-controlling changes of the sea." He died on July 7, 1975.

for observing developing storms. The war brought several changes to the field of meteorology; most significantly, practical weather forecasting became a priority. Though training meteorologists and providing weather information for the military consumed much of Bjerknes's time, he used the association to his advantage. With his son Jack's help, he set up a network of daily weather observations and measurements from hundreds of locations across Norway, justified by the valuable meteorological data to be supplied for military use. He retained military support even after the war, arguing that the government should play an active role in helping to alleviate the food shortages by providing a 24-hour weather forecasting service for the farmers. With the means to collect massive amounts of data from all over the country, the following years were very productive for Bjerknes and the other members of what came to be known as the Bergen School of Meteorology. Mapping the data graphically and combining the information with Bjerknes's circulation theorems provided insight as to how the atmosphere functioned.

The Bergen team's ongoing research revealed an overall picture of a patchwork atmosphere composed of constantly moving air masses. Depending on the conditions, different meteorological effects occurred at sites called discontinuities, where distinct air masses met. Knowledge of the existence of air masses with different characteristics permitted mathematical predictions of their movement based on physical principles, and therefore, the prediction of oncoming weather patterns. Bjerknes's mathematical models were too complex to predict weather rapidly enough for practical purposes without the aid of advanced computer technology, but he and his collaborators developed the concept of fronts from this data.

A front is the boundary between two air masses with different physical properties such as temperature and humidity. The Norwegian meteorologists adopted the military battle term *front* to describe the clash between two dissimilar large air masses that can result in violent weather. Because cold air is usually denser than comparatively warm air, the two masses do not mix upon meeting; the cold air slides underneath the warmer air, lifting the warmer air up. A *cold front* is when a wedge of cold air advances toward a mass of warm air, and a *warm front* is when warm air advances toward a mass of cold air. The passage of a front through an area can cause

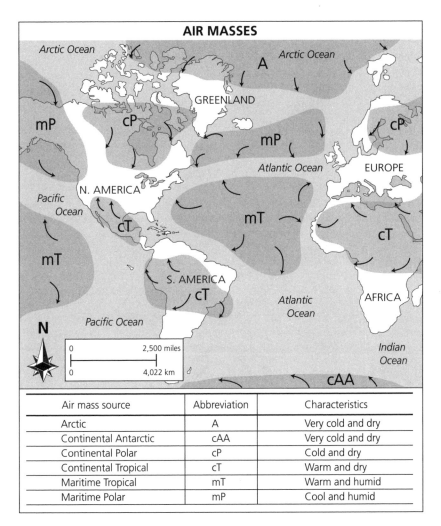

Air masses adopt the qualities of temperature and humidity characteristic to the region over which they form, but as the masses travel away from the source region, their properties gradually change.

dramatic changes to weather in the region, including cloud formation and precipitation.

The polar front is a semicontinuous transition zone that separates polar air masses that form at high altitudes and tropical air masses that form at middle latitudes, generally in between Alaska and southern Florida. In 1918, Jack Bjerknes had observed that

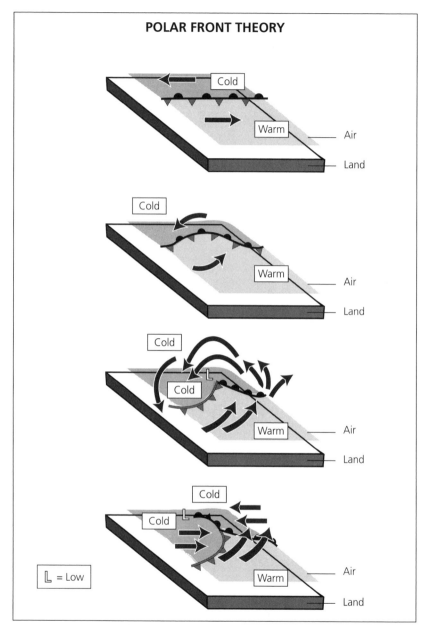

POLAR FRONT THEORY

Low-pressure systems form gradually at lines of convergence between cold and warm fronts. Wave formation leads to the development of counterclockwise currents of rising air that intensify until the cold front catches up with the edge of the warm front during occlusion.

low-pressure systems resulted from the convergence of two front lines that sandwiched a wave of warm air. The Bergen team built upon this foundation to develop the polar front theory (also called the Bergen cyclone model), describing the formation, progression, and dissipation of midlatitude cyclones.

At the polar front, easterly winds blowing cold air that originated at high altitudes meet warmer air blowing in the opposite direction. If stationary, little or no movement occurs; however, if disturbed by the flow of the *polar jet stream* or by an obstruction such as an elevation in the terrain, the frontal surface can become distorted. This leads to wave formation, a common event at the boundary where two moving fluids with different densities meet, such as when a breeze (the first fluid) blows over the surface of a lake (the second fluid). Cold air from the north pushes southward through the boundary, displacing warm air and frequently forming a V-shaped pattern. Warm air pushes northeast, forming a counter-clockwise circular current with an area of low pressure developing at the point of convergence. The phenomenon intensifies, and uplifting of warm air leads to cloud formation. Because the cold front travels faster than the warm front, the cold front eventually catches up with the warm front, closing the gap in a process called *occlusion.*

The classical model developed by the Bergen team described wave cyclones that originated at the polar front, but low-pressure systems can develop in other regions as well. Bjerknes summarized the results of two decades' worth of atmospheric research in *On the Dynamics of the Circular Vortex with Applications to the Atmosphere and to Atmospheric Vortex and Wave Motion* (1921). In this comprehensive work, he explained the nature of cyclones, the ideas of which remain mostly unchanged. He likened the behavior of air masses to the forces exerted by water in motion, such as waves, whirlpools, stream flow, and turbulence. The success of this classic book spread the new perception of meteorology as a science to countries far beyond Norway, including the United States. Knowledge of fronts gave meteorologists information about winds, temperature, clouds, and precipitation, all necessary for making accurate predictions of weather.

Father of Modern Meteorology

In 1926, Bjerknes accepted a professorship in mechanics and mathematical physics at his alma mater, renamed the University of Oslo, where he remained until his retirement in 1932. In the later years of his career, he taught theoretical physics, continued to study hydrodynamics, researched the nature of sunspots, wrote scientific books and articles, and continued to promote meteorology from a random collection of observations and haphazard speculation to a meaningful science.

In 1932, he served as president of the International Association of Meteorology and Atmospheric Sciences of the International Union of Geodesy and Geophysics. The National Academy of Sciences and the Royal Society of London inducted Bjerknes as a foreign member. He also belonged to the Norwegian Academy of Oslo, the Washington Academy of Science, the Dutch Academy of Science, the Prussian Academy, the Royal Society of Edinburgh, and the Pontifical Academy of Rome. Many universities awarded Bjerknes honorary degrees, and he received the Agassiz Medal for Oceanography, the Symons Medal for Meteorology, and the Buys-Ballot Medal for Meteorology. He died of heart failure on April 9, 1951, in Oslo, Norway. In his honor, in 1995, the Section on Oceans and Atmosphere of the European Geophysical Society established the Vilhelm Bjerknes Medal, awarded annually for distinguished research in the atmospheric sciences.

Bjerknes's aspiration was to transform meteorology into a respected scientific discipline, a goal achieved by the Bergen School of Meteorology during his lifetime. The military, agricultural, aviation, and fishing industries quickly came to depend on the practical applications of Bjerknes's research. His revolutionary idea of applying the physical principles of hydrodynamics and thermodynamics to the atmosphere improved the accuracy of weather forecasting and the prediction of long-term weather patterns. Meteorologists today use high-speed computers to perform numerical weather prediction based on Bjerknes's original attempts. These contributions, in addition to his work on the formation and behavior of cyclones, air masses, and fronts, all form the foundation for current theory and weather forecasting, earning Vilhelm Bjerknes the title "father of modern meteorology."

CHRONOLOGY

1862	Vilhelm Bjerknes is born on March 14 in Oslo, Norway
1880	Begins studies in mathematics and physics at the University of Kristiania
1888	Receives a master of science degree from the University of Kristiania
1889	Attends lecture series on electrodynamics given by Henri Poincaré in Paris
1890	Assists Heinrich Hertz on electrical resonance research in Bonn, Germany
1892	Completes a doctorate degree in physics from the University of Kristiania
1893	Obtains a position as lecturer at Stockholm's School of Engineering
1895	Becomes professor of applied mechanics and mathematical physics at the University of Stockholm
1897	Mathematically describes general circulation patterns of light (warm) and heavy (cold) fluids and applies the concept to the atmosphere
1904	Proposes system for numerical weather prediction
1905–41	Receives annual research stipend from the Carnegie Institute
1907	Returns to Norway to become professor of applied mechanics and mathematical physics at the University of Kristiania
1913	Accepts professorship in geophysics and founds the Geophysical Institute at the University of Leipzig in Germany

1917	Becomes professor of geophysics at the University of Bergen and founds the Geophysics Institute of Bergen in Norway
1921	Publishes the classic book *On the Dynamics of the Circular Vortex with Applications to the Atmosphere and to Atmospheric Vortex and Wave Motion,* describing air masses and fronts
1926	Becomes professor of mechanics and mathematical physics at the University of Oslo
1932	Retires from the University of Oslo
1951	Dies on April 9 of heart failure at the age of 89, in Oslo, Norway

FURTHER READING

Cox, John D. *Storm Watchers: The Turbulent History of Weather Prediction from Franklin's Kite to El Niño.* Hoboken, N.J.: John Wiley, 2002. Highlights the work of early weathermen and outlines the evolution of weather forecasting.

Earth Observatory, National Aeronautics and Space Administration. "On the Shoulders of Giants: Vilhelm Bjerknes." Available online. URL: http://earthobservatory.nasa.gov/Library/Giants/Bjerknes. Accessed February 9, 2005. Biographical profile of Bjerknes with links to biographies of other scientists who have made contributions to the understanding of the Earth's climate and environmental changes.

Ellavich, Marie C., ed. *Scientists: Their Lives and Works.* Vol. 4. Detroit: U*X*L, 1999. Alphabetically arranged introductions to the contributions of scientists from a variety of fields. Intended for middle school students.

Friedman, Robert Marc. *Appropriating the Weather: Vilhelm Bjerknes and the Construction of a Modern Meteorology.* Ithaca, N.Y.: Cornell University Press, 1989. An analysis of the revolution in theoretical and practical meteorology initiated by Bjerknes.

Gillispie, Charles C., ed. *Dictionary of Scientific Biography.* Vol. 2. New York: Scribner, 1970–76. Good source for facts concerning personal background and scientific accomplishments but assumes reader has basic knowledge of science.

Magill, Frank N., ed. *Dictionary of World Biography: The 20th Century.* Vol. 7. Pasadena, Calif.: Salem Press, 1999. Chronological arrangement of important world figures. Written for young adults.

Paul J. Crutzen

(1933–)

Paul Crutzen pioneered research in atmospheric chemistry that brought attention to the effect of human behavior on global climate. (© *The Nobel Foundation*)

Depletion of the Ozone Layer

Anyone who has ever slathered their skin with a layer of sunscreen lotion to prevent getting burnt by the Sun's ultraviolet rays owes a debt of gratitude to the atmospheric chemists who have worked hard to ensure human activities do not destroy the protective layer of ozone in the *stratosphere*. Though direct contact with ozone is dangerous to humans, mankind depends on the ozone in the stratosphere to absorb a large amount of the Sun's damaging *ultraviolet radiation* before it reaches the Earth's surface. Much of the current knowledge about the chemistry of the ozone layer is due to the research efforts of Paul Crutzen, a trained civil engineer who entered the workforce as a bridge builder in Amsterdam. Crutzen longed for a career in academic research, but unfortunate circumstances during his childhood, including effects of the war, illness, and being from a family of modest means, led him instead to a technical school for civil engineering. One day he applied for a position as a computer programmer for a meteorology research facility. He had no related experience but got the job, and as a result he became one of the world's most respected atmospheric chemists, earning the Nobel Prize in chemistry in 1995 for his work on processes that affect stratospheric ozone levels.

Hardships

Paul J. Crutzen was born on December 3, 1933, in Amsterdam, the Netherlands. His father, Jozef Crutzen, was a waiter, and his mother, Anna Gurk Crutzen, worked in a hospital kitchen. The Second World War (1939–45) caused shortages of food, water, and fuel and punctuated his elementary schooling. Despite the hardships, Paul progressed on schedule with special help from a teacher, passed the entrance exam for middle school in 1946, and prepared for entrance to the university by focusing on the natural sciences and mastering the French, English, and German languages. When he was not studying, he enjoyed playing soccer, chess, and ice skating on the Dutch canals and lakes. An unfortunate adverse reaction to a smallpox vaccination affected his performance on the final middle school exams, and as a result he did not qualify for a university stipend. His family's modest means could not support the cost of a university education, so Paul entered a technical school, where he received instruction in civil engineering in 1951.

In 1954, Crutzen met Terttu Soininen, a Finnish history and literature student from the University of Helsinki, while he was vacationing in Switzerland. They were married in 1958 and moved to Gävle, Sweden. Their first daughter, Ilona, was born in 1958, and their second, Sylvia, in 1964. Crutzen credits his devoted wife for his success by supporting his scientific studies.

The year he completed his civil engineering program, 1954, Crutzen got a job at the Bridge Construction Bureau of the City of Amsterdam. He worked on bridges and homes for four years, with a 21-month interruption to serve in the Netherlands military, but he wanted an academic career. In 1958, he responded to a solicitation for applications for a computer programming position in the department of meteorology of the Stockholm Högskola (became Stockholm University in 1961). Even though he had no experience, they hired him, and he moved to Stockholm in 1959.

A Second Career

As the home of the Meteorological Institute of Stockholm University (MISU), which had the fastest computers in the world, and the associated International Meteorological Institute (IMI), Stockholm was a hot spot for meteorological research. After his arrival, Crutzen mostly worked on developing the first numerical weather prediction models, but he also programmed a model of a tropical cyclone. Being employed at a university gave Crutzen the opportunity to attend lectures; however, his position could not accommodate the laboratory components of the physics and chemistry courses, so he became a theoretician rather than an experimentalist. By 1963, he completed the requirements for a *filosofie kandidat* degree (similar to a M.S.), with a concentration in mathematics, statistics, and meteorology. He continued his graduate studies in meteorology, choosing the topic of stratospheric ozone as his research focus.

Composed of approximately 78 percent nitrogen, 21 percent oxygen, and less than 1 percent argon, the atmosphere is roughly divided into four layers. The troposphere is the closest to the Earth's surface, followed by the stratosphere, the *mesosphere*, and the *thermosphere*, which is closest to the Sun. The stratosphere extends from about six to 30 miles (10–50 km) above the Earth's surface. The temperature of the stratosphere ranges from approximately –67°F (–55°C) in its lower region to around 28°F (–2.2°C) in its upper region. The difference is largely due to sunlight being absorbed by a form of oxygen known as ozone (O_3) as it passes through the stratosphere. Up to 90 percent of the atmosphere's O_3

is found in the stratosphere, forming a shield around the Earth that protects the *biosphere* from harmful ultraviolet radiation. After helping another scientist develop a computer model for the atmospheric distribution of oxygen *allotropes*, different forms of the same element, Crutzen became particularly interested in the *photochemistry* of ozone.

Photochemistry is the branch of chemistry dealing with the effect of light on chemical reactions. Light catalyzes some chemical reactions; for example, ultraviolet light breaks down diatomic oxygen (O_2), the allotrope of oxygen that humans depend on for respiration, into two singular atoms of oxygen (O). Because much ultraviolet radiation reaches the stratosphere, the concentration of monatomic oxygen is high, and it rapidly reacts with diatomic oxygen to create ozone. Ozone is a bluish gas with a distinct odor, and though in the troposphere it acts as an irritant to eyes, respiratory tracts, and skin, it also has the ability to absorb the ultraviolet radiation emitted from the Sun. Ultraviolet radiation is harmful to certain plants, damages eyes, mutates DNA, and causes skin cancer in humans; thus, human existence on Earth depends on the protection provided by the stratospheric ozone.

Crutzen examined the rates of the chemical reactions responsible for creating and breaking down ozone in order to explain its levels and distribution in the stratosphere. Ozone is constantly being created naturally in addition to being broken down. Because of its instability, a molecule of O_3 readily donates an oxygen atom to other molecules in the stratosphere. As long as ultraviolet radiation continues to break down other oxygen allotropes, free oxygen atoms are available to combine with diatomic oxygen (O_2) to recreate molecules of O_3 to maintain its concentration. Crutzen challenged the existing proposed rate constants, stating that they would lead to a rapid loss of ozone in the troposphere within days, and suggested that additional unexamined photochemical processes were important, including those involving nitrogen compounds. He also mentioned the unrecognized importance of a reaction between hydroxyl (OH) *radicals* and methane (CH_4). This work formed the dissertation for his *filosofie licentiat* degree (similar to a Ph.D.), which he received from Stockholm in 1968.

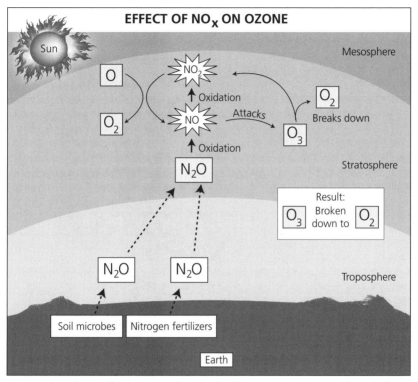

EFFECT OF NO$_X$ ON OZONE

Sun

Mesosphere

O

NO$_2$

↑ Oxidation

O$_2$

Breaks down

O$_2$

NO Attacks

O$_3$

↑ Oxidation

N$_2$O

Stratosphere

Result: O$_3$ Broken down to O$_2$

N$_2$O   N$_2$O

Troposphere

Soil microbes   Nitrogen fertilizers

Earth

N_2O produced by soil microorganisms makes its way to the stratosphere, where it oxidizes into ozone-destroying NO_X.

Believing the levels of nitrogen compounds in the stratosphere were connected to the ozone distribution, Crutzen worked on figuring the amounts of nitric acid (HNO_3) in the stratosphere as a postdoctoral fellow at the University of Oxford from 1969 to 1971. The presence of nitrogen oxides (NO_x), namely nitrogen monoxide (NO) and nitrogen dioxide (NO_2), turned out to be the most significant cause of ozone depletion in the stratosphere at altitudes between 15 and 28 miles (25 and 45 km). These NO_x form by the decay of dinitrogen monoxide (N_2O), more commonly known as nitrous oxide or laughing gas. Soil microorganisms are a major source of N_2O, as are nitrogen fertilizers. In the early 1970s, scientists were unaware of the steadily increasing levels of N_2O being released into the atmosphere. Crutzen published a paper in 1970, "The Influence of Nitrogen Oxides on the Atmospheric Ozone

Mario J. Molina

Mario José Molina was born on March 19, 1943, in Mexico City, Mexico. After receiving a degree in chemical engineering from the Universidad Nacional Autónoma de México (UNAM) in 1965, he traveled to Germany and studied the kinetics of polymerization at the University of Freiburg for two years. He returned to Mexico, where UNAM appointed him assistant professor of chemical engineering, and after one year, he moved to Berkeley, obtaining his Ph.D. in physical chemistry from the University of California (UC) in 1972. He remained at Berkeley for one year studying energy changes during chemical reactions and then transferred to UC at Irvine.

Working with the physical chemist F. Sherwood Rowland (1927–), Molina began researching a class of synthetic organic compounds called chlorofluorocarbons (CFCs). Crutzen's research demonstrating that nitrous oxide released by bacteria in the soil contributed to the breakdown of ozone molecules in the stratosphere caused Molina and Rowland to question whether man-made chemical pollutants had a similar effect. Industries used CFCs in products such as aerosol spray cans and refrigerants. Though CFCs are very stable in the troposphere, they found that in the upper atmosphere, ultraviolet radiation from the Sun broke down CFCs into chlorine, fluorine, and carbon atoms. After determining that each single atom of chlorine had the potential to catalyze the breakdown of 100,000 molecules of ozone, they suggested that the millions of tons of CFCs released into the atmosphere each year would rapidly deplete the protective ozone layer, threatening the Earth's biosphere. For this work, the Royal Swedish Academy of Sciences awarded Molina and Rowland the 1995 Nobel Prize in chemistry, to be shared with Crutzen. Most countries stopped producing CFCs by 1995, but preexisting CFCs will continue to affect the composition of the atmosphere for decades to come.

Molina was appointed to the faculty at UC at Irvine in 1974. He joined the molecular physics and chemistry section at the Jet Propulsion Laboratory of the California Institute of Technology in 1982 and was promoted to senior research scientist two years later. While there, he joined numerous other concerned atmospheric chemists who were examining the cause of the seasonal depletion of ozone over Antarctica. The Massachusetts Institute of Technology lured Molina away in 1989 with a joint appointment as a professor in the department of Earth, atmospheric, and planetary sciences and in the department of chemistry. He was named MIT Institute Professor in 1997. He continues to research chemistry of the atmosphere and the ways human behavior affects it.

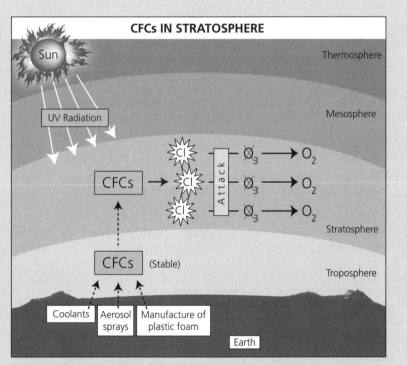

CFCs are stable in the troposphere, but in the stratosphere, ultraviolet radiation breaks them down, releasing chlorine atoms that contribute to ozone depletion.

Content," in the *Quarterly Journal of the Royal Meteorological Society*, describing the destructive effects of NO and NO_2 on ozone.

SSTs and Anthropogenic Chlorine

To Crutzen's dismay, others did not immediately recognize the significance of his findings or were choosing to ignore them, as was evidenced by a study sponsored by the Massachusetts Institute of Technology. The 1970 MIT report analyzed the impact of introducing large stratospheric fleets of supersonic aircraft and concluded that emissions of NO_x (and other compounds) by such aircraft were insignificant in ozone photochemistry, clearly contradicting Crutzen's findings that suggested it would have a destructive effect. This incited him to expand his studies on NO_x, hydrogen oxides, and HNO_3. Because his background was limited, Crutzen found it necessary to teach himself much of the chemistry necessary to understand his investigations. In December 1970, he submitted a paper demonstrating the seriousness of the problem of increasing NO_x in the stratosphere from supersonic stratospheric transport (SST). The paper, "Ozone Production Rates in an Oxygen-Hydrogen-Nitrogen Oxide Atmosphere," was not published in the *Journal of Geophysical Research* until October 1971, due to an extended mail strike in Britain at the time. That April, Professor Harold Johnston from the University of California at Berkeley had submitted a paper with similar findings that was published in August, two months before Crutzen's extensive study came out. Instead of getting upset at the delay in his own paper's publication, he was excited to have the backing of an eminent scientist.

In 1971, Crutzen returned to Stockholm University and continued his studies on NO_x. He submitted a dissertation titled, "On the Photochemistry of Ozone in the Stratosphere and Troposphere and Pollution of the Stratosphere by High-Flying Aircraft" to the University of Oxford in 1973 and obtained his doctor of science degree (more advanced than a Ph.D.). This topic became popular, and the National Academy of Sciences published a report summarizing the conclusions in 1975, confirming the destructive role of NO_x in stratospheric ozone chemistry.

Crutzen became increasingly interested in how human activities affected natural processes, such as the chemical reactions in the stratosphere. In fall 1973, he started looking for anthropogenic (resulting from human influence) sources of chlorine, an element that had been the focus of several recent studies related to ozone depletion. Two researchers from the University of California at Irvine, Mario Molina and Sherwood Rowland, sent Crutzen a preprint of a paper titled "Stratospheric Sink for Chlorofluoromethanes: Chlorine Atom-Catalyzed Destruction of the Ozone." Crutzen developed a computer model of chlorine in the stratosphere, and two months after the publication of Molina and Rowland's paper, he presented an analysis predicting that 40 percent of the ozone at 28 miles (40 km) would be destroyed by the continued promiscuous use of chlorofluorocarbons (CFCs). Two decades later, Crutzen, Molina, and Rowland shared the 1995 Nobel Prize in chemistry for their work that elucidated the chemical processes responsible for creating and destroying ozone.

Hole in the Ozone

Others recognized not only the significance of these findings, but also Crutzen's expertise in the new specialty of ozone depletion. The National Oceanic and Atmospheric Administration (NOAA) hired him to consult on stratospheric chemistry studies at their Aeronomy Laboratory in Boulder, Colorado, in 1974. He also started working part time for the Upper Atmosphere Research Project of the National Center for Atmospheric Research (NCAR), where he became director of the air quality division in 1977. Even as an administrator, he continued his research on chlorine-catalyzed ozone destruction and photochemical modeling, and he also initiated an interdisciplinary project examining the delicate balance of interactions of the atmosphere and the biosphere.

During the middle of the 1980s, Crutzen joined the effort to identify the cause of an ozone hole forming over Antarctica. In 1985, Joe Farman and his colleagues from the British Antarctic Survey published a critical report showing a sharp decline in ozone over Antarctica and noting a correlation between the decreased ozone levels and increased levels of stratospheric chlorine. The following year, one of Crutzen's former graduate students, Susan Solomon, hypothesized that chlorine became activated on the surface of ice particles that form clouds in the stratosphere over Antarctica. With Frank Arnold from the Max-Planck-Institute for Nuclear Physics in Heidelberg, Crutzen published a paper in *Nature* in 1986 titled "Nitric Acid Cloud Formation in the Cold Antarctic Stratosphere: A Major Cause for the Springtime 'Ozone Hole.' " The paper stated that the wet surfaces of the ice particles in the stratosphere catalyzed the transformation of inactive chlorine species (released from the action of ultraviolet radiation from the Sun on CFCs) into highly reactive radicals that created ozone-attacking molecules. To make matters worse, one of the created molecules, chlorine monoxide, reacts with other molecules to produce even more chlorine atoms, creating a positive feedback mechanism that accelerates ozone destruction.

Clear evidence has implicated man-made chlorine and bromine compounds as being responsible for originating the ozone-depleting processes. In 1987, members of the United Nations adopted the Montreal Protocol on Substances That Deplete the Ozone Layer to phase out the production and use of CFCs and other substances that release chlorine and bromine into the atmosphere. By 1996, the industrial world stopped producing these harmful substances that are expected to gradually disappear, allowing the ozone to recover by the middle of the 21st century. Scientists unfortunately have identified other atmospheric concerns, such as the increased emissions of greenhouse gases (GHGs).

Biomass Burning and Nuclear Winter

Amplified atmospheric levels of GHGs, including carbon dioxide (CO_2), methane (CH_4), dinitrogen monoxide (N_2O), and others, resulted in a *global warming* trend that began in the 1970s. Public awareness of the atmosphere's importance led to the consideration of the effects of tropical deforestation. Biomass burning is commonly performed in the tropics to convert forests for agricultural use, control insects and weeds, preserve pasturelands, and for other reasons. The procedure releases great quantities of GHGs as well as smoke particles into the atmosphere, significantly affecting its chemistry and the climate. Scientists believed the introduction of excess carbon dioxide and other carbon compounds into the atmosphere from the fires contributed to the greenhouse effect, leading to global warming. After happening upon a forest fire in Colorado in 1978, Crutzen collected air samples and performed chemical analyses to measure the amounts and ratios of the emitted gases. From this data he showed the gases comprised a large proportion of the total global emissions, a finding that stimulated further interest in the effect of GHGs released by biomass burning. Subsequent studies carried out by Crutzen and others showed that the release of large quantities of reactive trace gases such as hydrocarbons, carbon monoxide, and NO_x stimulated the formation of ozone during the dry season in the topics. Contrary to what they expected, pollution from biomass burning counteracted global warming rather than contributed to it. In 2002, scientists reported the results of an investigation into clouds of black carbon and sulfur dioxide over India from the burning of coal and oil. Results from their studies showed that solar heating was reduced significantly, canceling out the effect of global warming in many places. More recently, Crutzen showed that fires set to clear fields in Asia and Africa blotted out 10 to 15 percent of the Sun's rays. Though it may seem comforting to know that burning has prevented global warming from being worse than it is, Crutzen warns that, as the smoke cover diminishes, the greenhouse effect will intensify.

In 1981, the editor of *Ambio*, a journal published by the Royal Swedish Academy of Sciences that addresses factors influencing the environment, invited Crutzen to write an essay for a special issue on the consequences of nuclear war. Crutzen stated that the level of NO_x in the stratosphere would increase and result in ozone destruction, but he went further by discussing other effects of massive amounts of sooty smoke from the ensuing fires of lumber in urban environments, petroleum reserves, industrial facilities, and forests that would be ignited by a nuclear holocaust. The black soot would absorb a large proportion of incoming sunlight (current estimates suggest 50 percent), causing daytime darkness and lower temperatures on the Earth's surface. Computer modeling confirmed the overall effect of Crutzen's predictions. Popular scientist and author Carl Sagan developed Crutzen's suggestion of a "nuclear winter," speculating that temperatures would plummet 18–65°F (10–35°C), with significant consequences to agriculture worldwide. Sagan's assumptions were a bit farfetched and his predictions extreme, but studies have supported the fact that nuclear war would profoundly affect the Earth's atmosphere and climate. Crutzen contends that his notion of a nuclear winter was his greatest political, rather than scientific, accomplishment.

Honors and Impact

In 1980, Crutzen moved to Mainz, Germany, where he became the director of the atmospheric chemistry division of the Max-Planck-Institute for Chemistry. From 1983 to 1985, he served as executive director. He held a part-time professorship in the department of geophysical sciences at the University of Chicago from 1987 to 1991, and he has been a part-time professor at the Scripps Institution of Oceanography, part of the University of California at San Diego, since 1992. He was a part-time professor at the Utrecht University Institute for Marine and Atmospheric Science in the Netherlands from 1997 until he became emeritus in 2000, the same year he became emeritus at the Max-Planck-Institute.

Crutzen belongs to several scientific organizations and has served on more than 30 scientific advisory boards exploring issues related to the atmosphere. During his distinguished career, he has published more than 170 scientific articles and authored over 50 other research publications. In 2002, the Institute for Scientific Information in Philadelphia named Crutzen the most cited author in the geosciences worldwide, with 2,911 citations from 110 publications during the period 1991–2001. He has received 14 honorary doctorate degrees and numerous other honors including the Rolex-Discover Scientist of the Year Award in 1984, the Tyler Prize for the Environment in 1989, the Global Ozone Award for Outstanding Contribution for the Protection of the Ozone Layer from the United Nations Environment Program in 1995, the Order of Merit of the Federal Republic of Germany in 1996, and election to the Pontifical Academy of Sciences in 1996. His most notable achievement has been his 1995 Nobel Prize in chemistry that he shared with Molina and Rowland for their work in atmospheric chemistry.

In addition to elucidating the catalytic activity of NO_x on ozone, Paul Crutzen's research demonstrating a connection between the metabolism of soil microorganisms and the ozone layer encouraged a surge of research activity on biogeochemical cycles and climate. Crutzen continues his work on atmospheric chemistry at the Max-Planck-Institute in Mainz. A few years ago he coined the term *anthropocene* to describe the current geological epoch beginning just two centuries ago, characterized by significant geological and ecological changes as a result of the impact from the activities of the exploding human population. Crutzen is a modest man who is more concerned with elucidating the complex processes that occur in the atmosphere than receiving credit and praise for his accomplishments, but his fundamental work in atmospheric chemistry and his pioneering achievements in ozone chemistry directly impact all of the Earth's inhabitants, people and plants alike. In response to the results of his research, the international community now recognizes the potentially negative consequences of human behavior and has made global atmospheric studies a priority. The world has enacted positive changes to prevent human activities from destroying the Earth's invisible stratospheric guardian.

CHRONOLOGY

1933	Paul J. Crutzen is born on December 3 in Amsterdam, the Netherlands
1951–54	Studies civil engineering in Amsterdam
1954–58	Works for the Bridge Construction Bureau of the City of Amsterdam
1956–58	Serves in the Netherlands military service
1959–74	Holds various positions in the department of meteorology of Stockholm University, reaching the position of research associate professor
1963	Receives the equivalent of a master of science degree, with a concentration in mathematics, mathematical statistics, and meteorology, from Stockholm University

1968	Earns the equivalent of a Ph.D. in meteorology from Stockholm University with a dissertation on the photo-chemistry of stratospheric ozone
1969–71	Researches the effects of nitrogen compounds on ozone levels as a postdoctoral fellow at the University of Oxford, in England
1973	Earns doctor of science degree from Stockholm University for his dissertation on the destructive effects of supersonic stratospheric transports to the ozone
1974	Begins working as a research scientist for the Upper Atmosphere Project for NCAR and serving as consultant for the Aeronomy Laboratory of the Environmental Research Laboratories at the National Oceanic and Atmospheric Administration in Boulder, Colorado
1976–81	Is adjunct professor in the atmospheric sciences department at Colorado State University in Fort Collins
1977	The National Center for Atmospheric Research promotes Crutzen to senior scientist and director of the Air Quality Division
1980	Moves to Mainz, Germany, becomes member of the Max-Planck-Society for the Advancement of Science, and serves as director of the atmospheric chemistry division at the Max-Planck-Institute for Chemistry
1983–85	Serves as executive director at the Max-Planck-Institute for Chemistry
1987–91	Holds part-time professorship in the department of geo-physical sciences at the University of Chicago
1992	Scripps Institution of Oceanography of the University of California appoints Crutzen part-time professor
1995	Shares the Nobel Prize in chemistry with Mario J. Molina and F. Sherwood Rowland for their work in atmospheric chemistry, particularly concerning the formation and decomposition of ozone

| 1997-2000 | Holds part-time professorship at the Institute for Marine and Atmospheric Sciences of Utrecht University, in the Netherlands |
| 2000 | Becomes professor emeritus at the Max-Planck-Institute for Chemistry and Utrecht University |

FURTHER READING

Allaby, Michael. *Encyclopedia of Weather and Climate*. 2 vols. New York: Facts On File, 2001. Comprehensive reference of 4,000 entries encompassing important concepts and definitions, history of ideas, types of weather phenomena, and biographies.

Amato, Ivan, ed. *Science Pathways of Discovery*. New York: John Wiley, 2002. Contains essays written by one dozen accomplished scientists, including one coauthored by Crutzen, sketching the evolution of the atmospheric sciences.

Malmström, Bo G., ed. *Nobel Lectures, Chemistry 1991–1995*. Singapore: World Scientific Publishing, 1997. Part of a series that publishes the lectures given by Nobel laureates. Includes complete bibliographies.

Nobleprize.org. "The Nobel Prize in Chemistry 1995." Available online. URL: http://www.nobelprize.org/chemistry/laureates/1995. Last modified April 13, 2005. Contains links to the presentation speech, Crutzen's autobiography, curriculum vita, Nobel lecture, an interview, and an informational illustrated presentation.

Prof. Paul J. Crutzen. Available online. URL: http://www.mpch-mainz.mpg.de/~air/crutzen. Last modified February 22, 2002. Crutzen's home page at the Max-Planck-Institute for Chemistry.

Stiekel, Bettina, ed. *The Nobel Book of Answers*. New York: Atheneum Books for Young Readers, 2003. Compilation of 22 essays written by Nobel laureates, including Crutzen and Mario J. Molina, in response to questions posed by children, such as "What Is Air?" and "Why Is the Sky Blue?"

GLOSSARY

air the mixture of gases that make up the atmosphere

air mass a large body of air with homogenous properties such as temperature and humidity

air pressure the pressure of air due to the weight of air above it; also called atmospheric pressure

allotrope a structurally different form of an element, having different chemical and physical properties

anemometer a device that measures wind speed

aneroid barometer a very sensitive type of barometer made with a vacuum chamber that expands or contracts according to changes in air pressure

anthropocene name proposed by Paul Crutzen for the most recent geologic epoch beginning about 200 years ago and characterized by geological and ecological changes resulting from the influences of human activities

aphelion the position of a planet when it is farthest from the Sun

atmosphere the layers of air that surround the Earth

barometer a tool used to measure air pressure

Beaufort wind scale a system that estimates wind speed based on its effect on inanimate objects, such as sails, surface waters, or trees

biosphere the region of the Earth that supports life and includes part of the Earth, its waters, and its atmosphere

capacitor a device used for temporary storage of electrical energy; also called a condenser

celestial meridian an imaginary curved line above every point on the Earth, through which the Sun crosses once each day at noon as the Earth rotates on its axis

cell   in meteorology, a center of high or low pressure

charge   the electrical energy present in something due to the excess or deficiency of electrons

cirrus   light, fleecy, thin, hairlike clouds found at high altitudes

climate   the average weather conditions in an area over a long period of time

climatologist   one who studies climates

climatology   the study of climate

cold front   the leading edge of a moving mass of relatively colder air

condenser   a device that holds or stores a charge of electricity; also called a capacitor

conductor   something that transports an electric current, such as water or metal

convection   motions of a fluid resulting from warm portions rising and cool portions sinking

cumuliform   having the form of cumulus clouds

cumulus   white, fluffy clouds with a horizontal base and rounded masses on top

current   a flow of water or air in meteorology, or of electrical charges in physics

dew   water condensed on a surface

dew point   the temperature at which air becomes saturated with moisture and transforms vapor into a liquid

eccentricity   a deviation from a circular orbit

electrodynamics   the study of electrical currents

equator   an imaginary circle around the Earth that everywhere is equidistant from the two poles, dividing the surface of the Earth into the Northern and Southern Hemispheres

Ferrel cell   a cell present at middle latitudes in between polar cells and Hadley cells

front   a boundary between masses of air with different properties

frost point   the temperature at which air becomes saturated with moisture and transforms vapor into a solid

gas   a physical state of matter that expands indefinitely without containment, neither a liquid or a solid

glacier   a large mass of flowing ice

global warming an increase in the average temperature of the Earth's atmosphere as a result of increased concentrations of gases that absorb heat, such as carbon dioxide

greenhouse effect the warming of the Earth's atmosphere due to water vapor, carbon dioxide, and other gases in the atmosphere that absorb and reemit heat radiating from the Earth's surface

grounded in electricity, when a conductor is connected to the Earth so electricity passes into it

Gulf Stream a warm current of water in the Atlantic Ocean flowing from the Gulf of Mexico up the east coast of the United States and then across the Atlantic to Britain

Hadley cell a cell in mean global circulation driven by excess heating near the equator, consisting of warmed air at the equator moving upward then outward, reaching midlatitudes, cooling and sinking, and moving back toward the equator

heat island the atmosphere over an urban area that is warmer and drier than surrounding rural areas

humidity the amount of water vapor in the air

hydrodynamics the science that deals with the motion of and forces exerted by fluids

hydrographer one who studies hydrography

hydrography the scientific description and analysis of the physical conditions, boundaries, flow, and related characteristics of bodies of water

ice age a period in Earth's history during which glaciers covered much of the Earth's land

iceberg a large, floating mass of ice broken from a glacier

insulator a material that is a poor conductor of heat or electricity

interglacial occurring in between two glacial periods

jet stream a long, narrow, high-altitude current of high-speed winds

kinematics the study of pure motions without reference to the forces producing them

Leyden jar glass jar filled with water and coated with a thin foil used to store electric charges

lightning the visible effect of electrical discharges in the atmosphere

lightning rod   a metal rod that protects buildings from lightning by conducting lightning to the Earth

lines of convergence   the areas where two flows of air come together

line squall   a line of thunderstorms preceding a cold front

magnetism   the force that electric currents exert onto other electric currents; the ability to attract iron

maritime meteorology   meteorology as it relates to the sea

mercury barometer   a device that uses mercury to measure air pressure

mesosphere   the layer of atmosphere lying about 30–50 miles (50–80 km) from the Earth's surface

meteorologist   one who studies meteorology

meteorology   the study of the atmosphere and changes in the atmospheric conditions that affect weather

midlatitudes   latitudes from about 30 to 60 degrees north or south of the equator

moraine   an accumulation of earth and stones deposited by a glacier

nephology   the study of clouds

nimbus   gray rain cloud

occlusion   the end stage of a cyclone

ogive   alternate bands of light and dark on a glacier

orgographic lifting   a process that occurs when a mass of air encounters an elevated landmass, such as a mountain, and is forced to travel up the slope of the physical barrier

ozone   a form of oxygen containing three atoms per molecule; O_3

paleoclimatology   the study of the Earth's prehistoric climate and how it has changed over millions of years

perihelion   the position of a planet when it is closest to the Sun

photochemistry   the branch of chemistry that deals with the effect of light (radiant energy) in producing chemical reactions

polar cell   a portion of general atmospheric circulation occurring at high latitudes that consists of air moving away from the poles at low levels, reaching midlatitudes, and then moving back toward the poles

polar front   a front marking the boundary between cold air moving toward the equator and warm air over midlatitudes

polar jet stream   the jet stream that flows from west to east in the Northern Hemisphere

pole   either extremity of the Earth's axis

precipitation   any form of water such as rain or snow that falls from the atmosphere to the Earth

prime meridian   the meridian of zero degrees longitude from which other longitudes are determined

radical   in chemistry, an extremely reactive atom or group of atoms that has at least one unpaired electron

regelation   the melting of ice under pressure and subsequent refreezing

sidereal time   time measured by the apparent motion of the stars

smog   a thick haze caused by air pollution from smoke, automobile exhaust, and other contaminants in the atmosphere

spectrophotometer   a device that measures the relative intensities of light in different parts of a spectrum

spontaneous generation   the debunked theory that life arises from nonliving matter

static electricity   stationary charges of electricity

stratiform   arranged in layers

stratosphere   the layer of atmosphere lying about six to 30 miles (10–50 km) from the Earth's surface

stratus   flat, extended, sheetlike, low-level clouds

temperature   the degree of hotness or coldness of something

thermodynamics   the study of various forms of energy, especially heat and its relations and conversion to other forms

thermosphere   the uppermost layer of the atmosphere, beginning about 50 miles (80 km) up and extending hundreds of miles into space

three-cell model   a model for global air circulation that involves three average circulations, or cells, that carry warm air from the equator toward the poles and cold air from the poles toward the equator

trade wind   a belt of wind blowing toward the equator from the northeast or southeast

troposphere   the portion of the atmosphere where all life exists, extending from the Earth's surface an average of six miles (about

10 km) upward over the poles and 12 miles (about 20 km) over the equator

Tyndall effect the scattering of light by particles suspended in a liquid

Tyndallization a low-tech method for sterilizing media that involves inducing spores to germinate then killing the vegetative cells by heat treatment

ultraviolet radiation high-energy radiation, having wavelengths between 100–400 nanometers, that is harmful to living organisms

urban meteorology the study of weather and climate conditions in and around cities

vacuum a space completely empty of matter

vortex (plural **vortices**) a mass of fluid with a circular motion like a whirlpool, or a region within a body of fluid in which the fluid elements have an angular velocity

warm front the boundary between one mass of air and an advancing, relatively warmer mass of air

weather the condition of the atmosphere, especially with respect to temperature, humidity, precipitation, and cloudiness, at a certain place and time

wind the horizontal motion of air above the Earth's surface

FURTHER RESOURCES

Books

Aguado, Edward, and James E. Burt. *Understanding Weather and Climate.* 3rd ed. Upper Saddle River, N.J.: Pearson Education, 2004. College-level text written for students with little or no background in atmospheric science.

Allaby, Michael. *Dangerous Weather.* 8 vols. New York: Facts On File, 2003–04. Descriptions of dangerous weather occurrences, including blizzards, hurricanes, floods, and more. Written for grades six through 12.

———. *The Facts On File Weather and Climate Handbook.* New York: Facts On File, 2002. Convenient resource containing a glossary of terms, short biographical profiles of celebrated biologists, a chronology of events and discoveries, and useful charts and tables.

Burroughs, William J., Bob Crowder, Ted Robertson, Eleanor Vallier-Talbot, and Richard Whitaker. *Weather.* Alexandria, Va.: Time-Life Books, 1996. Covers the mechanics of weather events, cloud formations, and climate conditions.

Elsom, Derek. *Weather Explained.* New York: Henry Holt, 1997. Teaches the basics of weather and climate for middle school students.

Lynch, John. *The Weather.* Willowdale, Ontario: Firefly Books, 2002. Nicely illustrated volume covering every global weather phenomenon, linked to a Learning Channel series.

Mogil, H. Michael, and Barbara G. Levine. *The Amateur Meteorologist: Explorations and Investigations.* New York: Franklin Watts, 1993. A "how-to" book with introductory information, written for young adults.

The New Popular Book of Science. Vol. 2. Danbury, Conn.: Grolier, 2004. This volume encompassing the Earth sciences contains sections covering the atmosphere, several weather related phenomena, forecasting, and climates at a level appropriate for middle and high school students.

Prentice Hall Science Explorer: Weather and Climate. Upper Saddle, N.J.: Pearson–Prentice Hall, 2005. Brief and simple explanations of the atmosphere, weather factors and patterns, and climate. Written for middle school students.

Rittner, Don. *A to Z of Scientists in Weather and Climate.* New York: Facts On File, 2003. Profiles more than 115 scientists, discussing their research and contributions. Includes bibliography, glossary, cross-references, and chronology.

Stein, Paul. *Forecasting the Climate of the Future.* New York: Rosen, 2001. Discusses the challenges of weather forecasting and the role of computers in prediction of the weather and of future climate. Written for middle school students.

Stevens, William K. *The Change in the Weather: People, Weather, and the Science of Climate.* New York: Dell, 2001. A description of the past, present, and future of the science of climate written for nonscientists.

Internet Resources

American Meteorological Society. "A Career Guide for the Atmospheric Sciences." Available online. URL: http://www. ametsoc.org/atmoscareers. Accessed February 7, 2005. Advice on how to prepare for a career in meteorology including education, career opportunities, and the job market.

Climate. National Oceanic and Atmospheric Administration (NOAA). Available online. URL: http://www.noaa.gov/climate. html. Last updated December 6, 2004. Federal source for information concerning climate. Contains links to the NOAA organization homepages and archived data on climate.

Climate Kids. Southeast Regional Climate Center. Available online. URL: http://water.dnr.state.sc.us/climate/sercc/education/

education.html. Last updated January 19, 2005. Games, activities, and resources for kids of all ages.

Earth Observatory. National Aeronautics and Space Administration. Available online. URL: http://earthobservatory.nasa.gov. Accessed February 7, 2005. Click on the links "Atmosphere" and "Oceans" for numerous relevant references and features.

Franklin's Forecast. The Franklin Institute Online. Available online. URL: http://www.fi.edu/weather. Accessed February 7, 2005. Explore this site to find information on meteorological satellites, lightning, radar, weather events, and weather-related activities.

NOAA History: A Science Odyssey. National Oceanic and Atmospheric Administration (NOAA). Available online. URL: http://www.history.noaa.gov. Last updated September 2, 2004. Explore links "NOAA Legacy," the "Hall of Honor," "Profiles in Time," "Stories and Tales," "A Nation at War," "Tools of the Trade," and "Art and Poetry from NOAA's Archives," all related to the history of NOAA.

O'Connor, Neil F. *Weather Talk*. Available online. URL: http://pao.cnmoc.navy.mil/pao/Educate/WeatherTalk2/indexnew.htm. Accessed February 7, 2005. Nontechnical information on basic weather elements plus a link to information on careers in meteorology.

Office of Climate, Water, and Weather Services. National Weather Service (NWS) kid's page. Available online. URL: http://www.nws.noaa.gov/om/reachout/kidspage.shtml. Last updated May 14, 2003. Kid's page of the NWS with various resources on general weather info, dangerous weather, and safety tips.

One Sky Many Voices. University of Michigan. Available online. URL: http://groundhog.sprl.umich.edu. Accessed February 7, 2005. Web site for a program that explores basic weather concepts by gathering local data and comparing and communicating with scientists and peers.

Walker, Nick. *Weather Basics*. Available online. URL: http://www.wxdude.com/basics.html. Accessed February 7, 2005. An online textbook for kids written by a meteorologist with chapters on meteorology, various weather phenomena, the Sun, the seasons, and forecasting.

Weather. National Oceanic and Atmospheric Administration (NOAA). Available online. URL: http://www.noaa.gov/wx.html. Last updated August 26, 2004. Federal source for news and information concerning weather. Contains links to the National Weather Service and other NOAA organization home pages, hot topics about weather, and watches, warnings, and forecasts.

Weatherclassroom.com. The Weather Channel. Available online. URL: http://www.weatherclassroom.com/home_students.php. Accessed February 7, 2005. Extremely resourceful Web site with features including an online encyclopedia, a glossary, an interactive weather forecast, "Ask the Meteorologist," information on meteorological careers, and additional online resources.

Welcome to Study Hall. Atmospheric Radiation Measurement Program, Office of Science, U.S. Department of Energy (DOE). Available online. URL: http://education.arm.gov/studyhall.stm. Last updated June 21, 2004. Part of DOE's education and outreach program for children, this site contains information on global warming and climate change.

WW2010. The Weather World 2010 Project. Department of Atmospheric Sciences, University of Illinois at Urbana–Champaign. Available online. URL: http://ww2010.atmos.uiuc. edu. Accessed February 7, 2005. A comprehensive Earth sciences Web site that features current and archived weather data and educational material. Visit the online guide to meteorology for an introduction to basic weather terms and how to read weather maps.

Zeus' Web. Naval Meteorology and Oceanography Command. Available online. URL: http://pao.cnmoc.navy.mil/Educate/ zeus/index.htm. Accessed February 7, 2005. An entertaining educational site sponsored by the U.S. Navy that teaches about weather phenomena, weather myths, forecasting tools, and more.

Periodicals

Bulletin of the American Meteorological Society

Published by the American Meteorological Society
45 Beacon Street
Boston, MA 02108-3693

Telephone: (617) 227-2425
Monthly journal of the AMS, contains editorials, topical reports, articles, and more

Weather
Published by the Royal Meteorological Society
104 Oxford Road
Reading, Berkshire RG1 7LL UK
Telephone: 0118 956 8500
Written for anyone with an interest in weather and climate

Weatherwise
Published by Heldref Publications
1319 Eighteenth Street NW
Washington, DC 20036-1802
Telephone: (800) 365-9753
A nontechnical, bimonthly journal with articles about meteorology and climatology

Societies and Organizations

American Meteorological Society (www.ams.org) 45 Beacon Street, Boston, MA 02108-3693. Telephone: (617) 227-2425
For Spacious Skies (www.forspaciousskies.com) 54 Webb Street, Lexington, MA 02173. Telephone: (617) 862-4289
National Weather Association (www.nwas.org) 1697 Capri Way, Charlottesville, VA 22911-3534. Telephone: (434) 296-9966
Royal Meteorological Society (www.royal-met-soc.org.uk/rms.html) 104 Oxford Road, Reading, Berkshire RG1 7LL UK. Telephone: 0118 956 8500

INDEX

Italic page numbers indicate illustrations.

A

Abbe, Cleveland 83, xvi
Abbe, George Waldo 100
Abbe, Martha 108
abiogenesis 94–95
aerosol spray cans 134
Agassiz, Alexander 57
Agassiz, Louis 55, 55–71, 100, xv
Agassiz, Rodolphe 56
Agassiz, Rose Mayor 56
Agassiz Medal, Vilhelm Bjerknes receives 124
aircraft, supersonic 136
air masses 46, 80–81, 120, *121*
air pressure 1–2, 3, 5
Allen, William 29, 35
allotropes 132
almanacs 15–16
altitude, and air pressure 1
altocumulus clouds 37. *See also* clouds
altostratus clouds 37. *See also* clouds
anemometers 50
aneroid barometers 5
Antarctica 135, 137
anthropocene 141
aphelion 64
Apollo 11 vii
Aquilon, the 44
Aristotle 3
Armstrong, Neil vii
Arnold, Frank 138
Arrhenius, Svante August 90–91
atmosphere 3, 120, 131–138, *133*, xiii, xiv
atoms 20
axis, of Earth 64–66, *65*, 76

B

Ballot, Christoph H. D. Buys 79
Barnard, F. A. P. 105

barometer 3–6, *4*
  aneroid 5
Beagle, HMS 48
Beaufort, Daniel Augustus 42
Beaufort, Mary Waller 42
Beaufort, Sir Francis 34, *41*, 41–53, xv
Beaufort wind scale 34, 47–48, *48*, *49*
Bertie, Albermarle 43
biomass burning 138–139
biosphere 132, 134
Bjerknes, Carl A. 114
Bjerknes, Jacob 115, 118–119, 121
Bjerknes, Vilhelm *113*, 113–126, xvi
black carbon 139
Bonnevie, Honoria 115
Braun, Alexander 56
Braun, Cécile 57, 67
Brazilian Fishes (Agassiz) 57
Buckland, William 63

C

calculus 7–8
capacitors 19
carbon 134
carbon, black 139
carbon dioxide 91, 138
carbon monoxide 139
Cary, Elizabeth Cabot 67
Castelli, Benedetto 2
Cavalieri, Francesco Bonaventura 7
celestial meridian 106
cells, circulation 77, 78, *78*
Celsius, Anders 7
CFCs (chlorofluorocarbons) 134–135, *135*, 137, 138
charge 18
Charpentier, Jean de 58, 59, 61, 63
chloral 96
chlorine 134
chlorofluorocarbons (CFCs). *See* CFCs (chlorofluorocarbons)

Ciampoli, Giovanni 2
Cincinnati Observatory 101
cirro-cumulus clouds 31, 37. *See also* clouds
cirro-stratus clouds 31, 37. *See also* clouds
cirrus clouds 30, *31*, 37. *See also* clouds
Cleveland Abbe Award 108
climate, definition of 55, xiii
Climate of London, The (Howard) 34, 35
climatology, paleo- 68–70
clouds 29–33, 35, 37
cold front 120–123, *121*, *122*
Coleridge, Samuel Taylor 37
Colgate, Charlotte 100
Collinson, Peter 18, 21
computers 124
condenser 19
conductor 18
Constable, John 37
Constitutional Convention 23–24
consumption 28
Contributions to the Natural History of the United States (Agassiz) 67, 68
convection 11, 32–33, 79
convergence 33
convergence, lines of 117, 118
Copley Medal
  Louis Agassiz receives 67
  Ben Franklin receives 18
Coriolis, Gaspard-Gustave de 80
Coriolis effect 80–81, *81*
Crutzen, Anna Gurk 130
Crutzen, Ilona 130
Crutzen, Jozef 130
Crutzen, Paul *129*, 129–143, xvi
Crutzen, Sylvia 130
crystals 89
cumuliform clouds 37. *See also* clouds
cumulonimbus clouds 37. *See also* clouds

cumulo-stratus clouds 31. *See also* clouds
cumulus clouds 30, 37. *See also* clouds
current (electric) 20
currents, tidal 76
currents (ocean) 11, *22*, 22–23, 47, 77
Cuvier, Georges 57
cycloid 8
cyclones 77, 114, 118, 123, xiv

D
Daily Weather Bulletin 102, 104
Dalrymple, Alexander 46
Darwin, Charles 49, 67
data viii
Declaration of Independence 24
deep currents 47
Denham, Thomas 14
Devik, Olav M. 117
dew 31
dew point 32
diamagnetism 89
disasters, marine 104
discontinuities 120
dissociation 90
DNA, mutation of 132
Dogood, Silence 13
Dutch East India Company 43
Dynamic Meteorology and Hydrography (Bjerknes & Sandström) 117

E
Earth, motion of, and climate 64–66, *65*, 77
eccentricity, orbital 64
electricity 18–21
electricity, static 21
electrodynamics 114
electrolytes 90
electromagnetic waves 114
electrons 20
Eliot, Mariabella 29, 35
El Niño 119
equatorial region 77, 80, xiii
erratics 60
Espy, James P. 79
Études sur les glaciers (Studies on glaciers; Agassiz) 63
Experiments and Observations on Electricity (Franklin) 18

F
Fahrenheit, Daniel Gabriel 7, xv
Faraday, Michael 88

Ferdinando II (grand duke of Tuscany) 5–6
Ferrel, Benjamin 74
Ferrel, William 73–83, *83*, 102, xv
Ferrel cells 78, *78*
Ferrel's law 74
Ferret, the 44
fiber optics 96
fireplaces 16–18, *17*
Fitzroy, Robert 48, 49–50
Fleming, Sanford 107
floccosus clouds 34. *See also* clouds
fluids 115–116
fluorine 134
foghorns 94
Folger, Abiah 12
food spoilage 94–95
Forbes, James 63, 90
forecasting 45–46, 101–105, 116–117, 118, 120
forest fires 138–139
Forster, Thomas 34
fracture, of glacial ice 89
Franklin, Benjamin *11*, 11–25, xv
Franklin, Francis 15
Franklin, James 13
Franklin, Josiah 12, 22
Franklin, Sally 15
Franklin, William 19
Franklin stove 16–18, *17*
Fredrikssteen, the 48
frontal lifting 33
fronts 120–123, *121*, *122*, xiv
frost point 32
Fujita, Tetsuya Theodore 52
Fujita tornado scale 52

G
Galilei, Galileo 2–3
geometry 7–8
glaciers 58–63, 66, 89–90
Glaciers of the Alps (Tyndall) 90
GlaxoSmithKline 29
global warming 138
Goethe, Wolfgang von 37
Great Ice Age 62
greenhouse effect 90–92
greenhouse gases 138
Gulf Stream *22*, 22–23

H
Hadley cells 78, *78*
Hamilton, Louisa 96
heating 16–18, *17*
heat islands 34
heat radiation 88, 90–92
Hertz, Heinrich 114

Hesselberg, Theodor 117
Howard, Luke 27, 27–38, xv
Howard, Robert 28
Humboldt, Alexander von 57, 66
hurricanes *49*
hydrodynamics 9, 113–114, 115–116
hydrography 42, 51
hydroxyl radicals 132
hypothesis viii

I
ice 58–63, 66, 89–90
ice ages 62, 69–71
icebergs 59
ice caps 59, *69*
ice sheets 59
ichthyology 56
indivisibles 7
ionization 90

J
jet stream 119
jet stream, polar 123
Johnson, Lyndon 119
Johnston, Harold 136

K
Keimer, Samuel 14, 15
Keith, William 14
kinematics 117
kites 107–108
Koren, Aletta 114

L
Lamarck, Jean-Baptiste 32
Laplace, Simon 75, 76–77
Latona, the 43
Leatham, Elizabeth 28
lens making 8
Leyden jar 18–19, *19*
lifting, frontal 33
lifting, orgographic 33
light 5, 91–94, *92*, *94*, 132
lighthouses 94
lightning 12, 19–21
lightning rod 20
lines of convergence 117, 118
line squalls 117
low pressure systems *122*
Lyell, Charles 58, 62

M
Mach, Ernst 9
magnetism 5, 89
Marcellus Hartley Gold Medal, Cleveland Abbe receives 108
marine disasters 104

maritime meteorology 42
mathematics 6–8
Maury, Matthew Fontaine 50–51
Maxwell, James Clerk 114
Méchanique céleste (Celestial mechanics; Laplace) 75
Mendenhall, Thomas Corwin 109
mercury 3, 6
Meredith, Hugh 15
meridian, celestial 106
mesosphere 131
meteorology xiv–xv
meteorology, maritime 42
meteorology, urban 34
methane 132, 138
microorganisms, soil 141
Mid-Atlantic Ridge 51
midnight 106
Milankovitch, Milutin 64, 66
Milankovitch weather cycles 65
millibars 4
Molina, Mario J. 134–135, 137
Monthly Weather Review 107
Moon 75, 76
moraines 60, *60*
Morris, James Nicoll 44
Murchison, Roderick 63
Myer, Albert 105

N
Nansen, Fridtjof 117
NASA vii
National Medal of Science, Jacob Bjerknes receives 119
National Weather Service 104–105
nephology 30. *See also* clouds
New England Courant (newspaper) 13
newspaper publishing 13, 15–16
Newton, Isaac 75
nimbostratus clouds 37. *See also* clouds
nimbus clouds 30, 31. *See also* clouds
nitrogen compounds 133, 136–137
Nobel Prize
    Paul Crutzen receives 130, 134
    Mario J. Molina receives 134
    F. Sherwood Rowland receives 134
nonconductors 20
northeaster 18

Northern Hemisphere, air masses in 80
nuclear war 139–140
nuclear winter 139–140

O
occlusion 123
ocean currents 11, *22*, 22–23, 47, 77
oceanic temperature 119
ogives 63
old wive's tales xiii
On the Dynamics of the Circular Vortex with Applications to the Atmosphere and to Atmospheric Vortex and Wave Motion (Bjerknes) 123
Opera geometrica (Geometric work; Torricelli) 7, 8
orbit, of Earth 64–66, *65*, 106, xiii
orographic lifting 33
oxygen 132
ozone 91, 129–130, 131–138, *133*, 134–135, *135*

P
paleoclimatology 68–70
parabolic motion 8
Pascal, Blaise 5
Pasteur, Louis 95
Pennsylvania fireplace 16–18, *17*
Pennsylvania Gazette 15
Percival, Margaret Augusta 108
perihelion 64
Phaeton, the 44
photochemistry 132–133, *133*
Physical Geography of the Sea, The (Maury) 51, 77
planus clouds 34. *See also* clouds
poetry 37
Poincaré, Henri 114
polar cells 78, *78*
polar front 121–123, *122*
polar ice cap *69*
polar jet stream 123
poles 77
pollution 34, 93, 134–135, *135. See also* ozone
Poor Richard's Almanack 15–16
Popular Essays on the Movements of the Atmosphere (Ferrel) 82
Popular Treatise on the Winds, A (Ferrel) 82
prime meridian 107
Principia (Mathematical Principles of Natural Philosophy; Newton) 75

printing 13
protons 20
Pulkova Observatory 101

R
radiant heat 90–92
rain 118
Read, Deborah 15
Recent Advances in Meteorology (Ferrel) 82
Récherches sur les poisons fossiles (Research on fossil fish; Agassiz) 58
regelation 89–90
reporting, weather 45–46, 101–105, 116–117, 118, 120
Researches about Atmospheric Phenomena (Howard) 34
Roberval, Gilles Personne de 8
rotation, of Earth 77
Rowland, F. Sherwood 134, 137
Rumford Medal, John Tyndall receives 93

S
Saffir, Herbert 52
Saffir/Simpson scale 52
Sagan, Carl 139–140
Sandström, Johann Wilhelm 117
San Josef, the 44
science vii
scientific method vii–viii
Seven Lectures in Meteorology (Howard) 33, xv
Shelley, Percy Bysshe 37
sidereal time 106
Simpson, Robert 52
Sims, Ollive 29
skin cancer 129, 132
sky, color of 91–94, *92, 94*
Smeaton, John 46
smog 34, 93
soil microorganisms 141
Soininen, Terttu 130
solar eclipse 74
Southern Hemisphere, air masses in 80
spaceflight vii
spectrophotometer 91
spontaneous generation 94–95
static electricity 21
sterilization 95
Stopford, Robert 44
storms 18, 79–80, 102, 117, xiv
stratiform clouds 37. *See also* clouds

stratocumulus clouds *36*, 37.
  See also clouds
stratosphere 129–130, 131,
  135, 138
stratus clouds 30–31. *See also*
  clouds
sulfur dioxide 139
Sun, heat from xiii
sunset 93–94, *94*
supersonic aircraft 136
surface currents 47
Symons Memorial Gold Medal
  Cleveland Abbe receives
    108
  Vilhelm Bjerknes receives
    124
Système glaciare (Ice systems;
  Agassiz) 63

T
telegraph 104
temperature, and liquid
  volume 6
*Temperature of the Atmosphere
  and the Earth's Surface*
  (Ferrel) 82
temperature scales 7
thermodynamics 113–114, 116
thermometer 6–7
thermosphere 131
three-cell model 78, *78*
thunder 21
thunderstorms 18, 79, 102,
  117, xiv
tidal currents 76

Tidal Researches (Ferrel) 79
tide-predicting machine 82
tides 75–77, 82
Tilloch, Alexander 31, 35
time, sidereal 106
time, standardization of
  105–107
time measurement 106
time zones 107
tornadoes 52
torr 4
Torricelli, Caterina 2
Torricelli, Evangelista *1*, 1–9,
  xv
Torricelli, Gaspare 2
Torricelli's barometer 3–6, *4*
Torricelli's theorem 8
trade winds 119
troposphere 32, 131
tuberculosis 28
turtle embryology 67
Tyndall, John *87*, 87–98, xvi
Tyndall, John, Sr. 88
Tyndall, Sarah Macassey 88
Tyndall effect 87, 91–94, *92*,
  94
Tyndallization 95

U
ultraviolet rays 129–130, 132,
  134–135, *135*
United States, founding of
  23–24
urban meteorology 34
Ussher, Henry 42

V
vacuum 3, 5
Venetz, Ignace 58, 63
Vilhelm Bjerknes Medal 124
volcanic eruptions 28
vortices 115

W
warm front 120–123, *121*, *122*
water vapor 88, 91–92, xiv
weather, definition of 55
weather map *103*
weather reporting 45–46,
  101–105, 116–117, 118, 120
whirlwinds 21
wind
  Beaufort's work on 41–42
  Bjerknes's work on 117
  Ferrel's work on 79
  overview of 46–47
  Torricelli's work on 8–9
wind circulation cell 77
wind scales 46, 52
Wollaston Medal, awarded to
  Louis Agassiz 58
Wollwich, the 47
World War II 130

PROPERTY OF FISCHER MIDDLE SCHOOL
1305 LONG GROVE DRIVE
AURORA, IL 60504